T0142431

Tomboy

Remembering a Family-Farm Childhood, 1934-1948

Virginia Evans McCormick

authorHOUSE®

AuthorHouse™
1663 Liberty Drive
Bloomington, IN 47403
www.authorhouse.com
Phone: 833-262-8899

Published by AuthorHouse 11/30/2021

ISBN: 978-1-6655-4437-5 (sc)
ISBN: 978-1-6655-4443-6 (e)

Print information available on the last page.

Images of Sharon View Farm and Evans family members are provided by the author. Images originally published in the Ayrshire Digest are reproduced with permission of the US Ayrshire Breeders' Association.

This book is printed on acid-free paper.

Contents

1

Birth Announcement In
The Ayrshire Digest

I was 86 years old before I saw my birth announcement in the *Ayrshire Digest*. Nothing unusual about that. I never knew I had one.

Making a trip down memory lane, I was browsing through an *Ayrshire Digest* in the archives of the Ayrshire Breeders' Association, which in recent years moved its headquarters to my hometown, Columbus, Ohio. In the December 1934 issue there it was!

A Daughter to Mr. and Mrs. Ellis Evans

Mr. and Mrs. Ellis Evans of Newark, Ohio, announce the birth in October of a daughter, named Virginia. Reports from Sharon View state that the household is operating on a twenty-four hour-a-day schedule, regardless of the code.

A Daughter to Mr. and Mrs. Ellis Evans

I laughed out loud. How fitting. Beyond his family, my father's herd of Ayrshire cattle was by far the most important thing in his life. But this was unusual. It was the only birth announcement I ever saw in the *Ayrshire Digest*, the official publication of the National Ayrshire Breeders' Association in Brandon, Vermont.

There is no one alive to ask, but I can guess why my birth announcement might have seemed appropriate to the editor of a journal devoted to news of award- winning cattle and association business. Mother told me several times that everyone was constantly trying to get her to sit down while my father was showing cattle at the Ohio State Fair six weeks before my birth in 1934. She was 4 ft. 11 in. tall, and I weighed nearly eight pounds at birth. She undoubtedly already looked like her first baby might arrive at any moment. But it was important for her to be there. Daddy was showing fifteen cattle at the fair, and was especially proud when his herd sire, Penshurst Great Star, won a banner with gold cord and tassels for Grand Champion Ayrshire Bull. That was great advertising for Sharon View Farm. Great Star got his picture in the *Digest* and a couple of months later my birth announcement rated two sentences.

I have often marveled at the apparent audacity of my parents starting a dairy business and a family at the height of the Great Depression. My birth announcement was simply official recognition of my entry into a twentieth- century version of that iconic institution, the family farm. This title usually referred to a farm that was owned and operated by a family, especially one that has been handed down from one generation to another. Family members contributed their labor and shared its economic rewards. I didn't know it then, but my childhood would coincide with agriculture's transition from family farms to corporate production units. This was a historic change in America's rural landscape, physically, economically, and socially.

No one grows up in the world she will live in at the age of thirty or fifty or seventy, but sometimes I suspect that my childhood experiences would seem as ancient and quaint to local third graders as the lives of the Pilgrims they study at Thanksgiving.

Even as I lived it, the world of my rural childhood was old-fashioned—a generation or two out-of-date by urban standards.

My parents' Ohio farm was not that nineteenth century self-sufficient family farm eulogized by modern editorial writers and movie directors who lament the demise of its self-sufficient pastoral perfection. I seriously doubt such images are any more real than the snowy wonderland one creates by inverting a glass ball to watch the drifting flakes descend on a trio of Christmas carolers.

During my childhood our farm was already reflecting the mid-twentieth-century trend toward specialization that would accelerate into the megafarm businesses of today. During the Great Depression and World War II, my parents' dairy farm was a comprehensive enterprise. It grew the crops that fed the cows, that produced the milk Sharon View Farm pasteurized, bottled, and delivered to customers on my father's milk route in town, and in aluminum cans to Denison University dormitories.

It was an operation that by necessity carried on seven days a week, three hundred and sixty-five days a year. But amazingly, in the early 1940s this one-hundred-acre farm supported our family (my parents, my brother and me, and widowed grandmother) our hired man's family; and the family of the man who operated the dairy pasteurizing and bottling operations in our milk house.

I neither expect nor wish for the resurrection of my childhood world, but sometimes my thoughts linger on the preparation it gave me—or failed to provide—for a world that includes internet communications, women's liberation, and global travels.

Throughout my sometimes isolated childhood, my private refuge was the space beneath the wisteria bush whose gnarled and twisted trunk enveloped our front porch. Retreating there with best friends like Jo Marsh from *Little Women,* or Anne Shirley of *Anne of Green Gables,* I explored wider worlds and dreamed of the future.

But I never came close to imagining reality.

2

A Buzzard's View

I never saw the farm where I grew up from the air—although I've lain on my back in the tall pasture grass and wished I could soar like the buzzards etching lazy circles in the air above me. With their huge wings extended five or six feet, they rode the air currents between the rolling hills with no apparent effort, their shadows creeping across the pasture as they completed each overlapping pass.

My father was wise in all matters pertaining to animal life, including these birds that some people call vultures. "They're hunting field mice or baby rabbits. That's what they like to eat."

I squinted my eyes, not really sure. "But if I can't see their eyes from the ground, how can they see a baby rabbit or a tiny mouse?"

My envy of the buzzards ended abruptly one day in that pasture. One of our cows had calved in the field, and there was a summer thunderstorm coming up. I rode with my father as he took the tractor and wagon to where the new mother was licking her wobbly-legged youngster, nudging him ever closer to her distended udder. I shooed her back with a stick while Daddy gathered the calf in his arms and deposited him on some straw in the wagon. He called for me to climb in and hold the calf still while we headed for the barn with the worried mother mooing and trotting along beside the wagon.

We had only gone a few yards, when four or five buzzards descended on the afterbirth, their wings flapping and hooked beaks tearing for a share of the bloody membrane. Shocked by their vicious fight but unable to look away from the disgusting display, I was amazed at how quickly they devoured their prize, heedless of the blood they splattered on their breasts. Well before we were out of sight, the afterbirth was devoured, and with a flap of their wings the big birds were again airborne.

Seeing my distress, my father sought to reassure me. "That's what buzzards do, honey. If an animal dies, a flock of buzzards will strip the carcass clean. That's God's way."

I snuggled the baby calf in my arms, allowing its furry head to hide my tears. Never again would I envy the buzzards. Nor would I ever again dare to lie still in the grass and watch them soar overhead.

But I know how my parents' farm might have appeared to the buzzards drifting over its fields. I have a photograph taken years later by an entrepreneur in a single engine plane—related no doubt to those who ply their trade on cruise ship gangplanks and dance floors, ever optimistic that the flattered egos of their subjects will yield a purchase.

And why wouldn't my father treasure an aerial view of Sharon View Farm? It was his pride and joy. Created by his grandparents, improved by his parents, it was his own birthplace, life work, and home for ninety years.

Aerial Photo of Sharon View Farm, c. 1960s

From birth to college this was my only home, a stability many of my contemporaries and most of today's youth find remarkable. The hundred acres of the farm my parents owned, bounded my early childhood world. It was a neat rectangle created by surveyors who disregarded the natural lines of the rolling hillsides that had been smoothed but not leveled by Ohio's final glacier. The total was divided into a checkerboard of rectangular fields, some long and narrow, others solidly square, but all changing from green to gold to brown with the seasons.

Sharon Valley Road, running northwest to southeast the six-mile length of the valley, neatly bisected our farm. In the 1940s, it had a gravel surface barely wide enough for two cars to pass, but perfectly adequate for the limited traffic of the farm families who lived on either side of us. If my father was on the tractor working in one of the fields by the road, or walking down the lane to the mailbox, he would throw his arm into the air, waving to any passing car, confident that it was someone he knew.

South of the road, near the farm's border, flowed a stream too small to warrant a name on maps, but large enough to provide a year-round source of water for livestock at pasture or children at play. Between this creek—or crick as we called it—and the road, were two flat fields my father considered his best bottom land for growing corn.

North of the road everything sloped gently uphill, with the central cluster of farm buildings bordered on three sides by fields whose crops rotated annually from alfalfa hay, to corn, to wheat. At the top of the hill, were two pastures where the white and rusty red of my father's Ayrshire cattle created a picturesque mosaic against the green grass—a rustic landscape that never failed to attract compliments from neighbors and visitors.

Here too, was a reliable spring that served both our house and barn. At the farthest end of the pasture stood a beach woods of stately gray trunks and drooping limbs whose shiny leaves created a magic space underneath that felt like the inside of a waterfall—glowing green throughout the summer and gleaming copper every autumn.

A gravel lane—we would never have presumed to call it a driveway—led uphill from Sharon Valley Road to the cluster of buildings where our family lived and worked. This site offered an excellent view of the valley, one more worthy of a landscaped English manor house than a collection of working barns and sheds.

The largest and grandest of these buildings was the big barn west of the house. Built in 1896 to replace one destroyed by fire when my father was a year old, it claimed a special place in his affections for their having grown up together. In my memory it was always neatly painted white and along the ridge of its slate roof there was usually a row of twenty or thirty plump pigeons resting comfortably like a chorus line waiting for the curtain to rise.

It was what farmers call a bank barn, nestled into the slope of the hill so that wagons circled around to the large sliding doors on the upper level and drove directly onto a heavy plank floor that resounded with a hollow thud from the hooves of a team of horses.

On this upper level, three hay mows filled the left side and offered an open chute in the center for pitching hay to the livestock below. On the right was a long corn crib, and behind it a feed room where sacks of ground feed waited to be dumped into the shaft that filled a wheeled cart below.

Beyond the feed room were two round silos so tall they topped the barn roof. These were filled late each summer with green cornstalks, freshly chopped, and seasoned with molasses.

Nestled into the curve of the embankment, beside the entrance to the barn's ground floor, was a cement block dairy building that my father built before I was born. An adjoining shed roof protected both the dairy entry and the door into the barn, and provided a covered space to park the dark-green paneled truck my father used to make deliveries on his milk route. On a summer day, the barn doors would stand open and the cows were up in the pasture until milking time. In the winter, you rolled the door aside and were assaulted by the misty warmth of the animals, the pungent smells of silage and manure, and a chorus of bawling calves who always proclaimed their hunger the minute a human arrived.

Cleanliness was of primary importance in a dairy barn. Floors were concrete that could be hosed down, and walls were whitewashed annually with a mixture of lime and water that left them sparkling white. On the west side of a center aisle that ran the length of the barn, were eighteen stanchions for milking cows who entered through a sliding door from the barnyard on the far side. Four additional stanchions in the center of the east side held four more cows and separated two pens for baby calves at the north end from two box stalls on the south end. One of these was solid concrete for the big bull with a ring in his nose, and the other a wooden stall that served as a maternity ward for any cow due to calve.

The barnyard on the south and west sides had a circular cement watering trough filled by water piped from the spring on the hill, and a wooden rack that, in the winter, was filled with hay before the cows were turned out for exercise while the barn was cleaned. In the spring, the cattle often churned the barnyard into a sea of mud that required knee high boots to wade across. In the summer, the cows headed immediately for their pasture and the area would be dry and vacant from morning until night.

Clustered beyond the barnyard were lesser buildings—a smaller barn with an attached shed that was the home of yearling heifers, the henhouse for mother's chickens, and nearest the house a combination garage and equipment shed.

Our house was a square frame two-story of no architectural distinction, but grandly described by architectural historians as the American Four Square. Like many farmhouses throughout the Midwest, it had evolved with the families who lived there. The original section was built in 1864 by my great-grandfather as a story and a half saltbox with its front entry flanked on either side by windows that overlooked an orchard of apple, peach and sour cherry trees between it and the road.

By the time I was born, all but a few fruit trees had died and been replaced by two fenced pasture lots for baby calves. Shortly after my grandparents' marriage in the 1890s, they raised the roof to a full two stories, and doubled its space with an addition to the rear. They enlarged its cellar to accommodate a new coal furnace that my father stoked daily throughout the winter.

When my parents were married in 1933, they divided both floors and converted one room into a kitchen to create a duplex with separate living spaces for our family and for my father's widowed mother. On the first floor we each had a living room, dining room, and kitchen. Upstairs we had four bedrooms and my grandmother had two bedrooms combined to form a large bedroom with a sitting area and walk-in closet. We shared the single bathroom with its porcelain bathtub resting on claw feet.

Grandma usually used the dogleg back stairs that went directly from her kitchen to her bedroom. But her living room also had a door to the front hall. The front stairs rose to a hallway that served all five bedrooms. It had a lovely cherry newel post and a banister polished by years of gliding hands—or the seats of our pants if no one was in sight to prevent our sliding down.

Beneath these stairs was the door to the cellar steps. If I was sent down to get a can of vegetables for mother, I would open the door carefully and reach for the string that pulled on the light bulb that cast a dim glow over the steps. I usually paused to listen carefully before venturing into this region of spiders and mice.

Although my brother Dave and I had never seen one personally, we were pretty sure we heard monsters down there—noises that Daddy assured us were just the furnace expanding and contracting as the fire burned. Sometimes we went down with him and watched him open the black iron door and shovel coal from the big pile onto the fiery red coals glowing inside. The furnace monster never made loud noises when Daddy was there.

On the other side of the cellar—we never called this dirt-floored space a basement—the stone walls were lined with heavy wooden shelves filled with rows and rows of glass jars that in the dim light gleamed like jewels with their golden corn and peaches; ruby red cherries, tomatoes, and beets; emerald green beans and cucumber pickles; or strawberry, raspberry, and blackberry jam. This represented the bounty of our garden and Mother's many hours over the big canning kettle that made the kitchen drip with steam.

Visitors approached our house by opening the metal gate in the wire fence that kept chickens out of the dooryard. Company came up the right side of the Y-shaped walk to the front door that was sheltered by a large porch with a wisteria vine that shaded much of its south side. The rest of us turned left and used the side entry that faced the barn. Most of the yard fence was hidden by shrubs and perennials—peonies, iris, lilies, and lilacs together with climbing roses, Rose of Sharon, and mock orange bushes that always needed a good pruning. The house itself was shaded on all sides by maple trees—except for one aged sour cherry tree outside the dining room window whose limbs began only about three feet from the ground. It was here, that my brother and I learned to climb almost as soon as we could walk.

On the north side of the yard was a vegetable garden about half the size of a high-school football field. Although Victory Gardens were essential during World War II, our family had long been nearly self-sufficient in producing fruits and vegetables. Along the entire length of the north fence were clumps of rhubarb and asparagus that were safe from the annual plowing and sent up new shoots every spring. On the east end, was a large strawberry patch that constantly replenished itself with runners bearing new little plants. The rest, my father or the hired man plowed every spring, walking behind a horse that pulled a single-bottom plow.

Rows in this plowed section were rotated from year to year in the belief that this foiled harmful insects. This space invariably included tomatoes, cucumbers, summer squash, lima and green beans, peas, beets, carrots, radishes, onions, leaf lettuce, cabbages and cantaloupes—which in our neighborhood we always called muskmelons. We never grew, and I never tasted, such exotic vegetables as broccoli, eggplants, or Brussel sprouts

Sharon View Farm was nearly equidistant from Newark, the county seat four miles to the east, and Granville, a college town four miles to the west. We went to Newark to pay taxes at the courthouse, shop for school clothes at Carrolls' or King's department stores, or pick up meat from the frozen-food locker my parents rented in a building near the railroad tracks.

Because Daddy's milk route customers were in Granville and we were members of the Granville Baptist Church, someone was there several days a week. This was where Mother dropped me off at the library while she shopped at Fuller's Market, Taylor's Drugstore, or Gregory's Hardware. We were comfortable in both communities but we didn't exactly belong to either one, a fact that became increasingly evident to me as I attended the Newark Township School and the Granville Baptist Youth Fellowship with completely different sets of friends.

3

Ellis and Helen

Sometimes I imagine my birth October 10, 1934 as an act of defiance—my parents thumbing their noses at the Great Depression.

In truth, I suspect that they were simply a young couple doing what young couples have always done. Their marriage the year before, and their audacious optimism in launching their dairy business, came only weeks after President Franklin Roosevelt's inaugural speech admonishing his countrymen that the only thing they had to fear was fear itself. Hordes of unemployed persons haunted every city and town as my parents were deciding to start a family and a new business, but they certainly weren't doing it for Mr. Roosevelt. Both came from families with a long Republican tradition, and my mother so hated FDR that she would stand and argue with his fireside chats on the radio.

Ellis Evans, 1913 Newark High; Helen Gebby,
1927 Miami University graduate

My parents—Ellis Evans and Helen Gebby—were always Mother
and Daddy. Even in adulthood we never spoke casually of Mom and
Dad, or any quaint variation such as Mama and Papa. Their choice? I
presume so, although I'm not sure that children are particularly aware
of such distinctions. I don't recall that we ever questioned who our
parents were. They were simply there—a reliable, all important presence
in our lives.

Married at the ages of thirty-eight and thirty-three, they were older
than the parents of most of my friends. I'm sure my birth was anticipated
with joy, but I continue to marvel at their leap of faith at a time when the
national birthrate was falling dramatically as economically devastated
young people postponed parenthood.

Perhaps it seemed to be now or never for this dutiful oldest son
of a widowed mother and the sheltered only daughter, who had
tasted independence and married late. Perhaps it was simply human
optimism—confident about new beginnings, and believing that even
though others might fail they would surely succeed through hard work.

Like most parents then and now, I'm certain they believed they could make things better for their children.

My father died six weeks short of his ninetieth birthday after living his entire life in the farmhouse his grandfather built. Sharon View Farm was his world. What I, and many others, would have found confining brought him continuing satisfaction and even that rarest of commodities, happiness. Some people skate smoothly across the surface of life's experiences leaving barely a trace of their passing, but my father savored each vivid detail of his world, and tucked it away in memories to be drawn out and enjoyed whenever and however he wished.

Many were the times I heard him respond to an observation or question with a line or stanza of poetry he had memorized decades earlier in his one-room school. And etched upon my own memory, are the nights we would finish the chores and head from the barn to the house, my childish legs taking two steps to each one of his. He often paused to relish the starry sky above, naming and pointing so that I might see the wide spectrum of constellations with such fascinating names—Aries the ram, Sagittarius the archer, or Taurus the bull. Try as I might, it was hard to see the shapes, even when he lifted me to his shoulder so that I could be at eye level with his pointing finger. Something in his heritage or his childhood experience gave him a zest for seeing, really seeing the details, and appreciating his world. When he studied astronomy in high school he remembered constellations for a lifetime.

When he was in his mid-eighties, I attempted to record something of my father's life story, and began by asking about his earliest memories. *"One of the first things I can remember was a cold winter day when my father had new baby pigs at the barn. I was just a little boy and the snow was pretty deep, but I begged and begged to go to the barn to see the baby pigs. Finally my father bundled me all up and carried me through the snow to the barn where the two sows had their babies. 'Old Poland China' had ten and 'Old Berkshire' nine. When my father turned the sows out for a drink, I could pet the babies. When you touched them they just quivered all over and ducked under the rest of the babies to hide. When my father picked one up so I could hold it, I remember being surprised how very heavy it was. It looked so soft."* When my father remembered baby pigs, he remembered exactly how many there were and what their mothers' names were.

My husband contends that my father had a Welsh trait for telling "shaggy dog" stories that ran on and on, but I believe the essence of my father's satisfaction with his life lay in the details of such compelling images that were collected and maintained for more than eighty years.

He was a man of average height for his generation, about five foot eight, and his stocky build was accented by the blue denim bib overalls that were his daily attire for work around the farm. These were always accompanied by a long-sleeved blue cotton work shirt with sleeves rolled to the elbows during the summer, allowing his muscular forearms to burn a mahogany red that contrasted dramatically with the milky white skin of his upper arms. I inherited this Celtic coloring and share the same tendency to sunburn. A second line of demarcation was the straight white line across his forehead created by the wide-brimmed straw hat that he wore all summer.

But sunburn lines were concealed when he donned his "uniform" for delivering milk in Granville. This was a long-sleeved gray twill shirt and slacks and a dark cap with a plastic-backed visor that he gallantly tipped to women customers. I remember riding with him one day as a small child of three or four and waiting in the truck while he carried bottles to the door of a regular patron. He evidently became engrossed in a lengthy conversation for I recall becoming very distressed that I had been abandoned, sure that he would never return, and wondering how I could ever possibly find my way home. Then I saw his cap on the driver's seat where he had left it and felt calmly reassured that he would certainly come back for his cap. Such thoughts, of course, seem ridiculous from an adult perspective, but they illustrate my childhood impressions regarding the significance of my father's milk route and my image of him dressing up to perform that important role.

When my father completed his studies in the one-room school at the corner of the farm, he passed the Boxwell examination that Ohio required for anyone wishing to attend high school in the early years of the twentieth century. His teacher gave him a much-treasured gold pin to wear on his necktie and his parents gave him a two-dollar watch that he wore in his vest pocket through all four years at Newark High School. This was a fifteen to twenty minute ride on horseback and he had to allow time to stable "Old Maude" in a nearby barn before classes began. There were no big yellow school buses then for students who lived beyond walking distance.

During his senior year, he took the physics and chemistry that were required for the college preparatory course and managed to graduate in what he described as "the bottom of the top ten percent" of the eighty-five members of the class of 1913. My math might not survive the Boxwell examination, but knowing my father's specificity I suspect he ranked eighth among those eighty-five.

But college wasn't an option. His father was suffering severely from arthritis and told his eldest son he needed his help on the farm or it would—unthinkable thought—have to be sold.

But Ellis was lucky. The following year—determined to win the support of farmers who wielded disproportionate political clout in the state legislature—the Ohio State University launched a short course for young farmers that ran from mid-October to mid-March to conform to their relatively light workload between harvest and planting. Ellis enrolled, paying sixty dollars for tuition, books, and five months of room and board with a family near the campus.

Ohio State was only about thirty miles west of the Sharon Valley farm and he came home every weekend to help with farm chores. It cost sixty-five cents for the forty-five minute ride on the B. & O. (Baltimore and Ohio) Railroad, or fifty cents for the longer ride on the electric interurban car that stopped every time someone flagged it down. It traveled by way of Buckeye Lake—a recreational reservoir that had originally been created to serve the Ohio Canal.

This five-month agricultural course was one of the highlights of my father's life. He retained fond memories of classes with legendary professors now memorialized with names on Ohio State University streets and buildings. He also participated in the military drill that was required of all male students at the land-grant university, and marched for the governor's inauguration at the state capitol.

But his father's health was declining. Neither service in the World War that claimed the lives of a couple of his high school classmates, nor attending another much desired year at Ohio State were in his future.

He had always taken it for granted that he would farm someday. Under his father's guidance, he gained practical experience, progressing from typical childhood tasks like tying braces for shocks of corn, to a man's job wielding the sharp knife that cut the dry corn stalks and built the shock.

But my grandfather's specialty of raising and training livery horses was becoming obsolete. In his animal science classes at Ohio State, my father decided that diary was the business opportunity of the future. He used his agricultural engineering class with Professor Ives to draw plans to convert his father's horse barn into a dairy barn with stanchions on the ground floor, and a silo for the new technology of harvesting and storing green corn as silage that improved the cow's diet and her milk production.

My father's activities centered on his agricultural interests with memberships in the local Farm Bureau and the national Ayrshire

Breeders' Association, where he was proud that Sharon View Farm won a number of national awards.

The only vacation he ever took was in the 1940s. He broke a leg in an icy fall and used several days of recuperation on crutches to travel by train and visit three or four well known Ayrshire herds in eastern Pennsylvania and the Ayrshire Breeders' Association headquarters in Brandon, Vermont—like a devout Muslim making the pilgrimage to Mecca.

Daddy was not a political or civic activist. The only leadership positions I remember him serving were as a deacon in our Granville Baptist Church and president of the Newark Township School Board. I am certain both were accepted from a sense of duty rather than personal ambition or status.

By the time I was eleven, I had outgrown my petite mother who never measured quite five feet. As I continued to grow inch by inch, by comparison I felt even more ungainly than the typical adolescent. But finally, in college, I had two roommates who topped my five foot six by several inches and left me feeling quite normal.

Mother was an energetic dynamo as impulsive as my father was calm. After graduating from Bellefontaine High School in 1918, she attended the county teachers' institute and was certified to teach in a local one-room school. After doing this for three years, she enrolled in the two-year Teachers' College at Miami University and received her certificate in 1923. She returned to teach two additional years at Bellefontaine, but having become an accomplished seamstress under her mother's guidance, she returned to Miami to become qualified to teach domestic science at the high school level. She received her bachelor's degree in 1927, earning her own way by supplementing the savings from her teaching years by waiting tables in East Hall. One friend who signed her yearbook marveled at the memory of four-foot, eleven-inch Helen carrying a dinner tray that seemed as long as she was tall.

While teaching at Bellefontaine High School, she attended the Ohio State University in the summer to qualify for teaching in the vocational program enacted by Congress in 1917 to provide special training for girls who were planning to be married and become full-time homemakers. In the 1920s this included most female high school students.

Vocational Home Economics was a landmark in recognizing the value of a woman's work in the home and the need for special education to perform it efficiently and effectively.

From this experience, Helen was hired in 1931 by the Ohio State University as the Licking County Home Demonstration Agent at the magnificent Depression salary of $2400 (approximately $39,000 today). The Agricultural Extension Service, legislated by Congress in 1913, required land-grant colleges to serve rural families, the disadvantaged population of the early twentieth century.

Although she had lived away from home while attending college, and had earned enough to support herself for several years afterwards, moving a hundred miles from her family to live alone was a major step. At two hundred dollars per month she was one of the highest paid single woman in Newark.

I have a picture from this period that shows Mother's light brown hair bobbed in the latest fashion, emphasizing the pixie quality of her petite stature. She was the proud owner of a new Model A Ford which she drove to night meetings throughout the county with a revolver on the seat by her side—a gun her older brother Jerry had taught her how to use in case she ran into "moonshiners" along the back country roads. Of course, she never actually fired it, and I always harbored serious doubts about either her will or ability to do so.

Dollars were scarce among farm families in these early years of the Great Depression. Her classes for homemakers involved money-saving measures such as safe methods for canning home grown fruits and vegetables, and her popular clinics for refinishing and reupholstering furniture to make their homes more attractive.

Rocky Fork Creek rambled through a scenic area in the northeastern part of the county and here she and agents in nearby counties helped Ohio State establish "Camp Ohio" for 4-H Club members—creating meals from whatever produce the campers were able to bring from home and supervising swimming in a deep hole in the rocky stream.

Home Demonstration Agent Helen Gebby at Camp Ohio, 1932

One week each summer was set aside for "Women's Camp," a rare vacation for farm wives in those Depression years. I have a picture of her with this group, on her knees in the front row with a scarf tied jauntily around her head—a carefree, fun-loving woman quite different from the hard-working mother we children later knew.

It was inevitable that she would meet my father, a progressive young farmer who was participating in programs such as the Farm Bureau and TVA (Tennessee Valley Authority) soil conservation demonstrations. It seems inconceivable that both reached their thirties without some innocent amorous adventures, but neither ever admitted it to my brother or me.

It was certainly true that work left little time for romance. I know from the brief newspaper account, that their wedding was a simple ceremony at the minister's home in Newark, attended only by their parents. Ellis wore a new dark suit which became his church uniform for the next two decades. Helen wore a street-length dress she made herself in her favorite cornflower blue—one that remained wrapped in tissue paper in her cedar chest as long as she lived. They returned for a family dinner on the farm and began their married life without a honeymoon. The paper didn't say, and I never thought to ask, but it would be a safe wager that my father changed into his overalls and milked cows that evening.

Like most women of that day, Mother was required to quit work when she married. She became a full-time homemaker, mother, and the capable business manager for Sharon View Farm. She found time to participate in her church women's group, a garden club, and the American Association of University Women—which had programs she said stretched her mind and perhaps gave her status in a time and place where few women were college graduates.

For years she played cello with the Licking County Philharmonic Orchestra, an instrument she had learned from her father and played with a church group while in high school. Although she had grown up on a farm, and fully believed it offered the good life, her interests were eclectic and definitely not typical of most farm wives of the nineteen thirties and forties.

Mother with Jennie & Dave   Dave and I, 1937

I was nineteen months old when my brother David was born and named for his paternal grandfather and great-grandfather. I've been told that I considered him my personal doll baby and begged to hold him, but that my parents had to watch carefully or I would poke him in the eye to see him wrinkle up his face and cry. Fact or fiction, it seems an apt description for the conflicting emotions of love and competition that existed between Dave and me, and perhaps between most siblings.

I study our solemn expressions in the formal portrait that was taken as a Christmas present for our grandparents the year I was three. With legs crossed precisely like Hummel figurines on the edge of a shelf, we appear too angelic to be true. As the oldest I was frequently responsible for my brother. I learned quite early that adults found my blond hair and blue eyes symbols of innocence that I was free to exploit. When playing with the neighborhood gang, any mischief would be attributed to the boys and I could escape Scot free.

Daddy with baby Dave   Grandma holding baby Dave

My grandmother, Kittie Evans, lived on the other side of our house. She had a sense of reserve that I now attribute to her New England heritage. The relationship between her and my mother was civil but far from the warm devotion one hopes for between a mother and daughter-in-law.

Although I never discussed it with either of them, I suspect that both found it difficult to share my father's time and affection. As the oldest son, he had supported his invalid father and then his widowed mother during the twenty years between his high school graduation and marriage.

But the wife he chose had a very different personality and standard of housekeeping. Mother never worried about making a bed or washing dishes unless company was expected or we had run out of clean dishes or clothes. She often became engrossed in reading a book, or a decorating, or repair project, and completely forgot that it was time to prepare a meal, while Grandma took pride in an orderly and immaculate household.

Grandma was nearly as tall as my father and she liked nice things—quality dresses, and jewelry like the ladies pocket watch set with tiny opals and enameled flowers that she inherited from her Aunt Sadie and ultimately passed to me. I suspect that it was Grandma's 1939 Studebaker that created the need to build the garage/machinery shed, for her car was always carefully driven inside while our 1934 Plymouth usually sat in the farmyard.

I'm sure Grandma doted on us children for I have a photo of her proudly holding Dave all dressed up in a nice dress and bonnet when he was about six months old. But her New England reserve did not encourage climbing unto her lap for hugs. We were more often invited to sit in a chair and have a cookie—trying carefully not to drop crumbs while we ate. We did not wander freely on my grandmother's side of the house, but I have fond memories of her winding up her Victrola with its flaring horn to listen to favorites such as *Springtime in the Rockies* or *Listen to the Mocking Bird*. There was nothing quite as grand as Grandma's Victrola on our side of the house.

My maternal grandparents, Grandma and Grandpa Gebby, lived a hundred miles away near Bellefontaine, Ohio---a trip that required about three hours on two-lane roads through several small towns. Before the war, we might visit them a couple of times a year, making the round-trip in a day if my father was able to go, or staying overnight if Daddy had work that required he stay home. We looked forward to this because my Uncle Frank's family lived next door to my grandparents and our three cousins were just about our age. Their farm had wonderful places to play hide-and-seek in the barns and machinery sheds that were completely new to us.

The gas rationing of World War II brought such trips to a halt soon after Grandma Gebby died in the spring when I was seven years old. I'm sure we were sad and undoubtedly cried, but I'm ashamed to admit that my most vivid memory of her funeral is of Mother and Uncle Frank trying to accommodate all five cousins who insisted on riding in the undertaker's shiny black car that followed the hearse to the cemetery, and still find space for two adults to supervise our behavior.

This was the first time I had ever seen a dead person in a coffin, and I was very distressed to learn that death was something that happened to people, not just cats or cows. For quite some time afterward I was afraid to go to sleep for fear it would happen to me, or worse yet to Daddy and Mother and leave Dave and me all alone.

My father had two brothers, Uncle Louis and Uncle Doc—whose real name was Charles but no one ever called him that. Uncle Louis drove a truck and lived near town. I remember him as being gone much of the time. He and Aunt Dorothy had four daughters, who were teenagers when I was a toddler. When Mother and Daddy went to Farm Bureau or Country Cycle meetings, sometimes one of them would stay with Dave and me. No one ever used the word babysit that I can recall. By the time I was old enough to want friends to play with, these cousins were more interested in boys and dating. Our ages were an unbridgeable gap to friendship.

Uncle Doc's farm was on the next road over, but only a short walk across the fields and creek. He was crippled from a bout of polio that nearly killed him as a boy. He always walked with a cane and even then limped badly on his shorter leg and twisted foot. He was one of the first in our neighborhood to purchase a tractor. Using his strong arms to propel himself unto the seat, he became gloriously free to buzz anywhere at any speed. I am always reminded of him whenever I see a teenage paraplegic hot-dogging in a motorized wheelchair.

Uncle Doc could diagnose a mechanical problem and fix almost any piece of farm machinery, a process that completely baffled my father. Fortunately they often shared farm work and we all knew that when the mower, or hay loader, or reaper broke we should run to the phone and call Uncle Doc.

Uncle Doc and Aunt Gertrude did not have children, and while he was often at our house we rarely visited them. I guess my aunt suffered from depression, probably a condition that would be easily treatable today, but one that everyone then avoided talking about. I remember vividly the day that my parents hurried over to their house and when they came home simply told us that Aunt Gertrude had hanged herself from a tree in the orchard near their house. We were never to ask Uncle Doc about it and we were especially never to ask which tree it was because that would upset him. We children didn't go to that funeral.

4

⟞ ⟞⟞⟞◆⟞⟞⟞ ⟞

Hen Wlad Fy Nhadau — Land of my fathers

Mother's tone was sharp. "There are snakes in there and poison ivy."

Although she hadn't specifically banned it, Dave and I knew the abandoned church and the overgrown cemetery around it were out of bounds. She had warned us it was dangerous and we were supposed to have sense enough to stay out.

But it was an easy walk from our house. It was such a tempting target with a broken fence adjoining the pasture on the western side of our farm. Time and again the forbidden danger lured us.

During my childhood, the single-room church's siding had weathered to gray and panes of rippled glass suggested something moving inside its long-unused interior. A tangled mass of rangy grass, wild roses, and weeds concealed all but the tallest of the surrounding tombstones, but the largest was so clearly carved you could read its inscription from the road---EVANS—our name.

I visited that cemetery again shortly after my father died, and found the simple frame church gone—a vast emptiness in the landscape of my memory. Fifty years have turned the site into a neatly mowed graveyard in the midst of suburban development. There are few tombstones remaining, and only a couple of dark junipers reflect the burial ground's antiquity.

It is difficult to resurrect the irresistible attraction of twisted vines that my brother and I once pulled apart to discover stones with inscriptions in a mystical language we could not understand or pronounce. "Trefna dy canys, Tyddy ea mi byddilyn."—old-fashioned Welsh phrases that modern dictionaries provide insufficient help in translating. Even when a tombstone clearly cited dates of birth and death—"anayd, Hyd. 11, 1829; bu farw Chwef. 10, 1850"—the strangeness of the language evoked mystery.

Long after Welsh stone cutters mastered the English language, the nativity of the deceased continued to offer magical place names, "Susanna Jones, a native of Trefynog," "Eleanor Thomas born in Cemgllwydron," "William T. Williams, a native of Llanllawddsg." Such strings of consonants. How could anyone wrap their tongues around the syllables and pronounce these words?

I remember quizzing my father, "What does it mean?"

"I don't know, honey. Most of the old folks who knew Welsh died before I was a boy." But seeing my disappointment, he offered a compromise. "Grandma Mary taught me to count. Would you like to learn?"

"Oh yes!" Catching his hand to skip along as we walk, I repeat each word carefully, "Ein. . . dau. . . tri. . ." Finally I have it — with a sing-song chant, *"Ein dau, tri, pedwar, pump, chwech, saith, syth, naw, deg,"* I am rewarded by my father's broad smile.

Being Welsh was a significant part of my heritage. My immigrant great-great-grandparents settled in this valley exactly one hundred years before I was born. Their birthplace was proudly carved on their tombstone—Cilcennin Parish, Cardiganshire. I rolled the letters across my tongue with a Celtic lilt as my father did, Kill-ken-in, imagining their home as a mossy stone cottage with a thatched roof like a picture I had once seen in a book. Wales was a magical world and I was part of it.

Like an artist who paints only in pastels, the Welsh people have a limited palate of family surnames. For centuries they relied for identification upon a name and location such as Thomas of Bryn Du, or David of Gwynfor. When the British government mandated that every family have a surname, it was logical for the Welsh to adopt patronymics. The family of John's son became Jones rather than the Johnson more common in England, the family of Hugh's son Hughes, David's became Davis or Davies, Evan's Evans, Daniel's Daniels, and so forth. Sometimes it was simply the son's name combined with his father, such as John Thomas to identify John the son of Thomas.

Carmarthenshire, on the rugged northern shore of the Bristol Channel, is marked by scenic crags and steep ravines, a land suitable for grazing livestock and offering bits of tillable soil only along its streams. In the early part of the nineteenth century it was a region of slate quarries and tanneries, and home to independent craftsmen such as weavers, cobblers, and blacksmiths who were associated with self-sustaining villages. One less-than-charitable English writer described this rock-strewn countryside as "the fag-end of creation, the very rubbish of Noah's flood."

My great-great grandfather, John Evans was forty-one and his wife, Sarah Morgan, two years younger when they embarked for America with their eight oldest children, undoubtedly committing themselves to this perilous journey in search of better economic opportunities for these children.

When they were married March 25, 1814, by Rev. Timothy Evans of Cilcennin Parish, John gave his residence as Esgairwen, and Sarah was of Rhiwlas Uchaf, picturesque names but not actually villages—simply leasehold properties with one or more thatched-roof stone cottages and outbuildings. When their oldest daughter, Hannah, was baptized January 16, 1815, her father was identified as "John Evans of Swmarch, a smith." He was already developing the strong arms of the blacksmith who would establish a family of nine children in Sharon Valley. Five of them, including my great grandfather, died as young adults from the tuberculosis that flourished on immigrant ships.

There was much happening in New York City on July 1, 1833 when the barque *Devereaux* landed, disembarking its 467 passengers including my Evans ancestors. They were the families of twelve farmers, ten printers, eighteen masons, three smiths, six painters, five carpenters, and six shoemakers—working class immigrants with skills to offer the new world.

Weary from their two-month voyage and speaking only Welsh, I'm quite sure that they paid little attention to the performances of The Magic Flute at the Park Theatre or the exhibit of "Beasts, Birds, Fishes, Sea-Monsters, Reptiles, and Insects in all their varieties" advertised at the American Museum on Broadway. The museum's exhibit of "Fancy Glass Blowing, in all its astonishing wonders" cost twenty-five cents.

My ancestors probably had no idea that groups of Democratic-Republicans were just then meeting at Tammany Hall to consider Martin Van Buren as a successor to President Andrew Jackson. They were anxious to complete their journey to Ohio.

This involved a slow six-week trip up the Hudson River to Albany, across New York's Erie Canal to Buffalo, then by steamboat across Lake Erie to Cleveland, and south on the Ohio & Erie Canal. This was a far more comfortable journey than the wagons pioneers had used to cross the mountains a few years earlier, but canal travel was keyed to the walking pace of mules that towed barges from the adjacent towpath. It was possible to leave the slow moving boat to purchase eggs and vegetables from local farmers, particularly during the tedious process of passing through a lock. Restless children were probably free to walk the bank a while and perhaps pick a few blackberries.

The Evans family finally arrived near Newark and made contact with relatives with a wagon to carry their belongings to the Welsh Hills near Granville. This settlement of Welsh-speaking immigrants was more than thirty years old, and here John quickly found work as a blacksmith and wagon maker.

The journey from Great Britain that I can today complete by a trans-Atlantic plane flight between dawn and dusk, had taken my immigrant ancestors the entire spring and summer.

John Evans was a legend among his grandchildren, although only eight or ten were old enough to remember him personally. Stories told by his children to their children described hands so calloused from lifting the heavy blacksmith's sledge that he could carry coals of fire in his bare hands from the family hearth to his forge to start a fire.

In the one-room school my father attended, students memorized poetry that he could recite with flowing resonance more than fifty years later. I particularly remember the Longfellow poem that immortalized the village blacksmith under a spreading chestnut tree.

> *"Week in, week out, from morn till night,*
> *You can hear his bellows blow;*
> *You can hear him swing his heavy sledge,*
> *With measured beat and slow,*
> *Like a sexton ringing the village bell,*
> *When the evening sun is low."*

I can imagine the constant glowing flame and beads of sweat

dropping from his forehead. I don't know whether Daddy ever equated this tedious work with his own great-grandfather, but I later realized that at the very time Longfellow wrote of the village smithy John Evans was plying his trade in Sharon Valley, probably in a three-sided shed open to the elements in all seasons but convenient for local farmers bringing a horse to be shod.

I have no photograph of my great-great grandfather. He lived past the invention of the daguerreotype, but persons of his class rarely considered having their image made. The appearance of my father and his cousins leads me to imagine John Evans of average height and stocky build, with muscular arms and a ruddy Celtic complexion. He certainly was not afraid of hard work as he satisfied a pioneer community's constant demand for wagon wheel rims, farm tools, household utensils, fireplace cooking cranes, and of course, many horseshoes.

But the primary goal of my immigrant ancestors, like so many others, was to own land. The class system of their homeland had deeply inscribed the distinction between those who owned property and those who did not. The Welsh Hills community near Granville, Ohio was already heavily settled and land was becoming expensive when John and Sarah arrived. A little more than a year later, however, on October 2, 1834 John paid five hundred dollars for one hundred and eighty-five acres of virgin land a few miles east in Sharon Valley.

John and his two oldest sons, including my fourteen-year-old great-grandfather David, began by clearing its large maples and oaks, and erecting a dwelling, stable, and blacksmith shop. Within five years he paid off the complete price and his deed was recorded at the courthouse. John and Sarah had achieved their American dream. They were landowners free and clear, an impossible goal for a tenant farmer in their native Wales.

Before John's death in 1855, the family's four sons and three married daughters were established on farms the length of the valley. The Evans family had become part of the family-farm culture which spread across the nineteenth-century Midwest. Their children learned English, and a succession of their granddaughters taught in the one-room school my father attended on the eastern border of Sharon View Farm.

Land, school, and church were nearly simultaneous priorities for these Welsh immigrants.

My Evans ancestors were Welsh Calvinistic Methodists—a religious theology akin to modern Presbyterianism. During the early part of the nineteenth century the Methodist chapels across Wales set up schools to preserve the Welsh language so their countrymen could read the Bible in their own language.

There is no evidence that the family was persecuted by the Anglican Church for their religious beliefs. In fact, John and Sarah's marriage, and the baptisms of their eight children born in Wales, were recorded in the official Anglican parish registers shortly before their emigration. But this was a matter of legality rather than religious commitment to the Church of England. Perhaps they saw it as something of an insurance policy, recording themselves among the believers should the ocean voyage prove fatal.

A year after their arrival in the valley, in October 1835, John and Sarah were among the seventeen founding members of the Sharon Welsh Calvinistic Methodist Church, organized by a Welsh minister who walked over one hundred miles from Cincinnati for the occasion. John was chosen as one of the seven trustees—women could be members but not leaders—who signed the deed for the churchyard which was the fascination of my childhood.

The small congregation erected a simple space for worship, twenty-one by thirty feet with a single entry on its eastern gable end. It had none of the architectural embellishments such as a steeple that were common to the Anglican Church. The building was completed in 1837 at a cost of $321.89 plus volunteer labor. I can easily imagine John Evans crafting iron hinges for the plain door, or his sons John and David among young men splitting wooden shingles for the roof.

A history of the church written in the 1950s, by volunteers of the Cambrian Society in Granville, described the interior furnished with a wild cherry pulpit and chancel, walnut pews arranged around three sides of a central iron stove, walnut wainscoting on the lower walls with wooden pegs above to hang cloaks, and oil lamps set in tin reflector brackets to provide light for evening services. For nearly fifty years services flourished here in the Welsh language.

My only glimpse of that distant past came one Sunday October afternoon when I was a teenager. A Cambrian society of Welsh descendants in Granville was undertaking the church's restoration and I joined my father in the overflow crowd for its rededication. Someone had repaired and washed the old windows and sprays of autumn foliage caught the sunlight on the pulpit as a surprising number of those present were able to join in singing rousing verses of favorite Welsh hymns. My arms prickled with goose bumps and I was reminded of the scene in the movie *How Green Was My Valley* of weary black-faced coal miners singing as they streamed towards their homes. Welsh people had so few material possessions. Maybe that was the reason they poured their very souls into musical celebrations.

As a child I realized this graveyard held an irresistible fascination. Only years later did I began to understand the dream of my Welsh ancestors to become landowners, and the emotional ties that Sharon View Farm held for my father.

5

A House Without a Key

To a child, our house seemed huge. Dave and I each had our own bedrooms—large rooms about fourteen feet square with floors painted brown, the old boards so wide they cupped and made the rag rugs ripple.

Our furniture was all antique. My cherry bed with tall posts on each corner was designed to support a canopy. A dresser with four drawers that stuck in rainy weather, and a small table beside my bed with a lamp and my Bible completed my bedroom. A single light bulb with a rosy glass shade shaped like a tulip hung from a chain in the middle of the high ceiling. My clothes closet was so shallow that hangers couldn't be placed sideways but hung on five or six hooks across the back.

There was plenty of room to play during warm weather, with blocks and trucks on the floor of Dave's room or with paper dolls in mine. In the winter, the only heat came through registers that weren't connected to the furnace, but were simply holes in the floor with an iron grate to allow warm air to rise from the rooms below. Mother opened them when we went to bed and closed them in the morning, but our rooms were cold and we slept under heavy piles of blankets and quilts. On winter mornings there would be a forest of ice crystals on the inside of the windows which might get thicker for several days in a row until the sun finally came out and melted them. We'd grab our clothes and hurry down to the kitchen to wash our face and dress in its warmth.

Mother and Daddy's room was the same size, but it also held the cedar chest where Mother kept her treasures—her wedding dress, a bundle of letters tied with a ribbon that Daddy wrote to her before they were married, and some of our baby clothes. It was a special treat when Mother opened the chest and I could breathe in its lovely cedar aroma as she shook out items like the lacy baby dress and booties that tied with pink ribbon. "Can you believe that you could wear these when you were a tiny baby?" My fingers traced the crocheted booties with awe as I gave a smile of disbelief.

Our bathroom held a bathtub that stood on big claw feet, the toilet, and a porcelain sink that rose from a pedestal on the floor. Wainscoting painted a light blue circled the walls to a height of about four feet. Above that, as in every other room of the house, mother had papered the walls to hide the cracks and uneven places in the plaster. We had running cold water in the bathroom, and in the summer Mother would carry a teakettle full of boiling water upstairs and pour it into the bathtub to warm the water from the faucet for our Saturday night baths. We had never heard of showers, and no one thought it necessary to take a bath every day. In the winter we had to bathe in the warm kitchen.

Windows in every room upstairs and down had white net curtains with a ruffle around the edges and across the top. Mother had to wash these every spring and fall, starch them, iron them, and re-hang them with ruffled tie-backs that framed the windows with a cottage-style drape.

There were roller blinds that tended to stick when you pulled them down and then snapped to the top with a bang. We rarely pulled them.

Privacy wasn't an issue when there were no other houses within sight and the road was too far away for passing cars to pay attention. On a stormy night though, I would lie flat on my back and during lightning flashes watch the wind blow the branches outside. Then I sometimes pulled the shades to shut it all out.

Our three rooms downstairs were equally spacious. Both the living room and dining room had hardwood floors and Axminister carpets that my mother prized highly. Although we spent much time sprawled across their plush surface with our games and toys, and I admired their bright colors and bold designs, I was too young to understand the symbolic pleasure my mother gained from their broad-loomed elegance after knowing nothing in her own childhood but homemade rag rugs.

A corner fireplace in the living room was the only survivor from a central chimney that had originally served heating fireplaces in each room. My parents considered it an emergency or supplemental source of heat, not an aesthetic amenity. On the rare cold days when it was used, we burned coal that made a glowing and long-lasting fire.

Mostly, I remember its cherry mantel as a place to hang our Christmas stockings—always Daddy's brown speckled work socks with white heels and toes that looked like monkey faces when stuffed. They were much larger than any Dave or I owned. These would be filled with tangerines, peppermint candies wrapped in cellophane, and walnuts in their shells which would occupy much of our Christmas morning cracking and picking out their sweet meats.

An upright piano with a richly polished cherry case dominated the living room. Mother's, and later my own, cello rested beside it, in a nook between it and the fireplace corner. Play *She'll be Comin' Round the Mountain When She Comes* we'd beg, as we gathered round Mother at the piano to sing our favorites.

When I entered the second grade, she enrolled me for piano lessons with a friend in Granville, but my repetitions practice of scales was as mechanical as the metronome that ticked relentlessly by my side. I hated it, and my protests were long and loud. After a couple of years and many warnings that "You'll be sorry later in life," Mother relented and allowed me to switch to cello.

I liked this instrument's mellow tone, and the responsibility of sliding my fingers along the strings to create each perfectly pitched note myself rather than pound it out on a piano key. But most of all, I liked the idea that as soon as I was good enough I could join an orchestra. Mother was wrong. Orchestra participation gave me much joy during my high school and college years and I never looked back and wished that I played piano.

But today I wonder. If mother had played flute or bassoon, would that have been my instrument of choice? Was I really expressing my own preference or simply seeking approval for emulating a loved parent— completely unaware that she had taken the same path and followed her cello-playing father? So many significant life decisions are rooted in a past beyond our knowledge, and we end up playing a sport or musical instrument, choosing an occupation or a life partner without recognizing the subconscious influences.

Between the living room front windows was the walnut slant-top desk that served as the Sharon View Farm office, and the top was usually down and covered with papers waiting for attention.

Beneath a high row of four small windows that faced west toward the barn sat a mossy green couch with ribbed upholstery. This was so scratchy on my bare legs, I usually preferred to stretch out on the floor when I was reading a book or playing with my paper dolls.

Mother's favorite chair was a small armless rocker with a seat and back that she had upholstered in a woodsy scene of rich greens and browns. Beside it stood a double-lid sewing box filled with clothes to be mended on one side and sewing equipment on the other. If she had time to sit down in the evening, she would inevitably pick out a sock, insert her darning egg into its heel or toe, and begin darning the hole to return it to wearable condition. I smile at the memory and wonder if there is anyone who grew up during the Great Depression who does not remember the blisters created by lumpy darned socks.

Unlike most dining rooms today, ours was actually used by the whole family for dinner in the middle of the day and supper each evening. We had never heard of a meal called lunch. Of course, supper took place after chores were done and that might be as late as 9 PM in the summer, but more often than not we all sat down at the dining room table together for these two meals.

This was a round walnut table that was always covered by a tablecloth, usually a pastel rose, green or blue. Mother liked pastels. The table was surrounded by four cane-seated chairs that mother had refinished and caned. We learned early not to climb up and sit on our knees for that punched a hole in cane seats.

It was an extension table that could be pulled apart to fit in three boards that were stored in a closet upstairs, but I only remember this happening the few times that Uncle Frank's family, Mother's brother, came to visit. Then she took the company dishes with little pink flowers from the buffet and put out the silver-plated flatware that was stored in a velvet-lined chest with slots and elastic bands to hold each piece in place. The buffet was centered between two shallow built-in cupboards with semi-circular doors that displayed mother's very best platters and goblets.

My favorite place in the dining room was an old and badly scarred walnut chest that sat beneath the windows. This was our toy chest. When we were ordered to clean up for dinner we simply lifted its top lid and tossed in the toys which were scattered all over the floor. It was big enough for Dave or I to hide in during a game of hide and seek, but entirely too obvious by the time we were old enough to climb in by ourselves.

Like the room, the dining table a was multi-purpose piece of furniture that on rainy days could be converted to a fort or a playhouse by Mother tossing a blanket over it that extended to the floor. Then we raided the lower kitchen cabinets for bowls and pans that furnished our secret space quite nicely. It was the perfect pre-Sesame Street entertainment in the days before television.

As we grew older, the dining room table was the perfect setting for a game of Monopoly or card games like Old Maid—a child's version of Hearts where the object was to pass on the dreaded Old Maid card with a straight face. But my favorite card game was Authors, a game that required collecting matching pairs of famous authors like Louisa May Alcott or Charles Dickens. We recognized their pictures before we could read their names. I adored William Makepeace Thackeray—not that I had read any of his books, but what a wonderful name. Anyone named William Makepeace Thackeray deserved to be a famous writer.

Sometimes Mother played with us, but not Daddy. He usually read the *Ayrshire Digest* until bedtime, but he did enjoy a game of Dominos now and then, and when I was about eight or nine he taught me to play chess. He liked a game of strategy and I tried hard, without success, to beat him.

The hub of our house though was the kitchen, for that's where Mother was much of the time. Underneath a bank of four windows that gave her a view across fields that alternated between meadow, corn, and wheat, was a double-bowl porcelain sink with linoleum-covered counters topping the cabinets on either side. Dirty dishes usually accumulated in the sink and on the counters to be washed after supper in the evening.

By the time I was five or six and could stand on the wooden seat of a kitchen chair, I loved to help wash dishes in the soapy water on one side while Mother placed them in the drainer on the other side, rinsed them with boiling water from the teakettle, dried them, and replaced them in the cupboards.

This was a good time for questions because I had her full attention.

"There was a hen sitting under the lilac bush for the longest time and I couldn't shoo her away."

"I expect that's where she's decided to lay a bunch of eggs and hatch some baby chicks."

"How do the baby chicks get inside the eggs before she sits on them?"

"Well, the Daddy Rooster gives the Mother Hen a seed that's inside the egg she lays. Then she sits on the eggs and keeps them warm until they grow into baby chicks. When they are ready to come out, they use their beak to crack the shell and hop out."

I had to think about that for a minute. "So when we eat an egg it can't become a baby chick?"

"Well, not all eggs have the seed to become a baby chick. That happens mostly in the spring when you see the Mother Hens making nests and laying a whole batch of eggs."

A light dawned in my head. I had been fascinated by a little nest with three blue eggs that I found when I was climbing in the cherry tree. "Is that like the nest I found with the blue eggs?"

"Yes, that was a robin's nest. Chickens can't fly like robins but they're birds who lay eggs to raise baby birds."

I grinned. "Yeah. That's nice."

I didn't realize then how lucky I was to feel free to ask questions or to have a Mother with a knack for honest explanations on a child's level of understanding. I'm sure we talked more with our parents, and they with us, because we were together constantly and there were few other adults or children in our lives much of the time.

The other working parts of our kitchen included a long counter between upper and lower cabinets where Mother mixed the ingredients and rolled out pie crust with a wooden rolling pin on a board sprinkled with flour. Or she would attach the handle to the metal grinder, clamp it to a wooden board and grind meat for meatloaf. Sometimes she let me drop the chunks of meat into the cup on top but I had to be very careful not to let my fingers get too close.

Pies and meatloaf and anything else to be baked would be placed in the oven of the porcelain range with four gas burners on one side and the oven at the same height on the other. The other major piece of kitchen equipment was the refrigerator with big coils on top. I was young enough to have missed the era of iceboxes which had to be filled with blocks of ice and cleaned of the thawed water, but the shape of our refrigerator's interior was little changed. It had no freezing compartment with ice cube trays, no meat or vegetable drawers, no shelves on the door. The boxy interior did have a couple of wire shelves for our glass bottles of milk, covered bowls of cottage cheese or leftover vegetables.

The table where we ate breakfast and where I colored pictures or did schoolwork was covered with a flowered oilcloth that could be wiped clean. One side was against the wall and there was room for one chair on each end and two on the side with their backs to the kitchen. Above it, a shelf attached to the wall held the radio that brought Daddy the news and weather report in the mornings while he ate his cornflakes or oatmeal. That was early, before I got up.

After I started to school, he would call upstairs to wake me just before he left for the barn.

"Vir-gin-i-a. Time to get up or you'll miss the bus."

I hated my name. Daddy was the only one who ever called me Virginia—or the kids on the school bus when they wanted to tease me by singing "Carry me back to Ole Virginny."

I was named for Mother's favorite Aunt Jennie, and that's what she always called me. Why couldn't she have just named me Jennie officially?

The busiest day of all in the kitchen was wash day. Mother had a double-tub washing machine that sat on the back porch but was rolled into the kitchen on wash day and connected to the faucet over the sink with a hose. Dirty clothes and bedding were sorted into five or six piles by color and degree of dirt. As one tub was filled from the faucet, in went a teakettle of boiling water from the stove, some Fels Naptha soap and first the white sheets and pillow cases. It was fun to watch them wiggle in the soapy foam as the agitator in the middle of the tub stirred them.

Then Mother swung the wringer to the washer side and guided the sheets or garments between its two rollers with one hand while cranking the handle with the other, allowing the wet items to drop directly into the rinse water in the other tub. The procedure progressed from lightly soiled white sheets and pillow cases through tablecloths and dish towels, underwear, dresses and blouses, and finally to Daddy's overalls. All went through the same wash and rinse water—with the addition of more hot water and soap as needed. It would be an ugly gray by the time Daddy's overalls with specks of manure around the bottoms of the legs went in.

After coming from the rinse water and through the wringer to make them as dry as possible, wet garments were carried in a large wicker basket to the clothes lines in the back yard. These metal lines had to be wiped clean and then everything fastened to them with wooden clothes pins whose round heads looked like little people. A pole with a forked end propped up the middle of the line, and as the heavy wet sheets went on it was gradually moved closer under the line to raise it higher and keep them out of the dirt. On a windy summer day it was great fun to watch the arms of shirts and legs of pants fill with the breeze and begin dancing.

But they had better be tightly clipped at the hems or they would drop in the dirt and have to go back and be washed all over again. And you always had to be on the lookout for a quick summer shower. Then Mother, Grandma and I would dash for the clothes lines, stripping off pins and dropping clothes into the basket as quickly as possible—dry or not. On cold winter days everything froze. Even before you finished pinning them, pants would swing stiffly like wooden puppet legs. I always found it amazing that clothes could go directly from frozen solid to dry.

Of course everything was 100% cotton and everything but underwear, socks, and Daddy's overalls had to be ironed. When Mother brought clothes in from the lines in the backyard, she sprinkled them with water, rolled them and piled them on the counter near the breakfast table to be ironed between other chores over the next day or two. Yes, she had an electric iron but this was long before steam irons were invented. When she wanted to press wrinkles from Daddy's good wool suit, she wet a piece of cloth torn from an old sheet, placed that on the inside of the wrinkled jacket, then put a dry cloth on top before ironing all layers.

It was in the kitchen, where messes could be tolerated that I had my first Toni home permanent, designed to make me beautiful for my eighth grade graduation.

My baby-fine straight hair was the bane of my childhood. How I envied friends with thick curls that never limped in wind and rain.

Sometimes Mother braided my hair into pigtails that began high on the side of my head and angled diagonally into plaits that fell over my shoulders. It was excruciating as she pulled the wisps tightly into place and wrapped the ends with a rubber band.

How well I remember the day in fifth grade when Stewart Beck—who sat behind me—caught one of my pigtails in the hole on his desktop designed to hold a bottle of ink. He could reach through his desk and gradually pull my pigtail further and further until I was practically lying in my seat, all the while smiling at Mrs. Callander so she wouldn't see what was going on and rap his knuckles with her ruler.

Pigtails were fine for most days, but graduation was special and Mother promised that I could have a Toni—like the beautiful girls in the newspaper ads. She bought the box that had special plastic curlers, bottles of solution, and tissue papers to wrap the ends of my hair onto the rollers. I wore my oldest blouse and shorts and draped a towel around my shoulders, but the solution still dripped and stung my scalp, and the fumes gave both of us teary eyes. After all of the curlers were rolled, Mother had to soak each one again with cotton balls dipped into the solution. I tried to keep it out of my eyes with a wash cloth and watched in amazement as it turned purple.

Then you sat and waited for the solution to work with Mother partially unrolling a roller after fifteen or twenty minutes to test how the curl was coming. When she deemed it ready, I held my head under the faucet at the kitchen sink to rinse away the curling solution, and Mother repeated the drippy process with cotton balls and a bottle of neutralizer designed to set the curl. Another wait, and finally she gently unrolled my new curls. After again rinsing under the faucet and wrapping my head in a towel, what fun it was to shake my head and watch my new curls bounce. It wouldn't last long, but for the moment I was ecstatic—a real woman, willing to undergo torture in the quest of beauty.

As I remember, something was always going on at our house. In an era before automatic washers, dryers, and dishwashers, and meals were prepared from scratch three times a day, something was probably always going on. Our house was never locked for the simple reason that we didn't own a key. Day or night, someone was always home.

6

Queens of the Farm

Their curving horns weren't really queenly crowns on their heads, but Ayrshire cows ruled our days. Nothing was more important than the morning and evening milking seven days a week, three hundred and sixty-five days a year. Miss a milking or two, and cows will go dry.

My father bought his first purebred Ayrshire cattle before he was married and I sometimes felt he put them first, even before Mother and Dave and me. In many ways they were his children too. He knew each one by name, recognized their personality quirks, and sensed any illness or injury. Visiting cattle buyers were amazed by the way my father—and even we children—walked calmly through the pasture among our 1000 to 1200 pound cows, patting their sides as they stoically chewed their cuds, feeling no fear of their sharply pointed horns.

I was too young to remember Queen of Maples, the first Ayrshire cow that Daddy bought at a local auction in the spring of 1919. He paid $175—a value that would equal at least $1750 in modern dollars. But I heard him tell the story until I knew it by heart. This special cow became his foundation for building a nationally recognized dairy herd.

She gave birth to twelve calves, eight of them daughters who exceeded or nearly equaled her lifetime production of 110,042 pounds of milk —enough for every child in an elementary school of 500 students to have a half-pint carton of milk every school day for over two years. Daddy may have made a lucky choice, but this was an impressive record in the 1920s.

That same fall he traveled east to visit Strathglass Farm north of New York City and Penshurst Farm near Philadelphia, large herds he had seen win awards at the Ohio State Fair. Both were owned by gentlemen farmers who had earned their money elsewhere and were setting production records by hiring managers to supervise milking large herds of more than one hundred cows three times a day. Daddy wanted the best, but their cattle were too expensive. He became friends with the veterinarian at Penshurst who suggested a good small herd nearby where he bought two cows, five heifers and a bull calf for $1700 and shipped them back to Ohio by rail. That was the beginning.

Sharon View Ayrshire herd in pasture, Ellis Evans by fence

By the time he had these paid for, Penshurst Man of War had emerged as the best Ayrshire sire in the country — something like a Kentucky Derby winner to purebred horse breeders. Daddy asked his veterinarian friend at Penshurst to pick out a son of Man of War for him, and by mail he bought Penshurst Romeo and a couple of years later a half-brother, Penshurst Noble—paying $200 for each when most bull calves sold for $50 to $75.

He smiled at me as he remembered this. "We got a 'lucky nick.'"

I didn't understand. "What's a 'lucky nick.'"

"Well, I heard a professor from the University of Illinois one time say it was like taking fifty apples from a barrel that had seventy good ones and thirty rotten apples. If you picked out forty-nine perfect apples that was a 'lucky nick'---better than fifty-fifty."

I thought about that for a minute. "So what's that got to do with calves?"

"Well sometimes a bull and certain cows produce calves one after another that are exceptionally good. I guess Penshurst Noble and the daughters of Queen of Maples produced a 'lucky nick.'"

I grinned. "I guess a 'lucky nick' is better than plain good luck."

If there were a king among the Ayrshires on our farm, it was of course our herd sire—the dangerous bull who lived in the concrete box stall. When Daddy or Willis, our hired man, took him out for a drink of water from the concrete trough just outside his stall, we were to stay a safe distance away and not jump or make a loud noise that would scare him. They never took him out of the stall without first clamping a metal pole onto the ring in his nostrils to lead him by his sensitive nose, keeping another pole in the other hand to nudge and guide him. More than one dairy farmer was seriously injured or killed when gored by their angry bull.

But in the days before artificial insemination, a resident herd sire was essential and the quality of his calves could make or break a farm's reputation. The genetics of purebred livestock was still in its infancy in those days. Before buying a new bull calf—as he did every two or three years because you shouldn't breed a bull to his own daughters—Daddy always pored over his *Ayrshire Digest* to analyze various bloodlines and weigh the potential characteristics that would provide the best body conformation and highest production of milk and butterfat when bred to the cows in his herd.

Buying an outstanding bull calf was the cheapest way to develop a high quality herd because his daughters carried his genes. In the 1930s Penhurst was the outstanding Ayrshire herd in the country. It was owned by Percival Roberts, who became wealthy merging his local steel bridge company with U.S. Steel. He built a 75-room mansion that became a legend of the Philadelphia Main Line and the more than 500 acre Penhurst Farm with elaborate barns supported a herd of over 100 Ayrshires milked three times a day by dozens of farm workers.

Penhurst Great Star, 1934 Grand Champion
Ayrshire bull, Ohio State Fair

Once you had a good herd sire it was excellent advertising to show him off. Great Star, the bull who won grand champion at the Ohio State Fair the year I was born, was a grandson of Penshurst Man of War.

When one of the cows came into heat, Daddy always sent me to the house while he took the bull out to breed her. I can't remember exactly how old Dave was when he was first allowed to stay and watch, perhaps six or seven, but I felt cheated that although I was a year and a half older I was a girl and it wasn't considered proper for me to stay.

So the next time I was sent to the house, I detoured up to the hay mow where I could lie on my stomach and peer through the hole that the men used to toss down hay. This was near the stanchions on the east side of the barn and by keeping very quiet I had a front row seat. I wasn't surprised to see the bull mount the cow's rear end—I had seen heifers to that to each other in the field when one was ready to breed—but I was shocked by the long pink thing the bull stuck into the cow's rear end. I had sometimes seen him flick it in and out while drinking at the water trough, but I had no idea it could become so huge!

Mother and I soon had a talk about penises and the fact that all male animals, including boys, used them to plant the seed that would make a baby grow. But we also talked about the difference between people and animals, and the aspects of love that made sexual intercourse so much more than just a physical act of procreation that all animals experience. Growing up on a farm provided valuable opportunities that are unavailable to modern sex education classes.

Actually I knew about birth well before I knew about conception. Baby calves and kittens were constantly being born on the farm. I can remember straightening out the gang about where babies come from during school recess with the authority of one who had witnessed many births. Usually a cow about to calve was placed in the stall in the barn rather than being let out to pasture, so if there were any problems Daddy could help her or call the veterinarian. But, like human mothers, a cow in labor can take quite a while. From an early age it was often my job to keep an eye on her and call Daddy from work if necessary.

A cow about to calve would usually pace the stall, lie down, then get up and pace some more before lying down for the birth. The first thing you could see would be the hooves of the calf's front feet, incredibly clean and black inside their protective sack. If you could see both feet it practically always meant that everything was going to be fine and you simply waited for the nose to appear. Then with a swish the whole calf would slide out and the cow would jump up mooing loudly to reassure it and begin licking its face to remove the sticky membrane.

If you only saw one foot and the cow was pacing and bawling, it was time to call Daddy. Sometimes he could roll up his sleeve and push his arm inside and find the leg that was doubled over and straighten it out, but sometimes he would have to call Doc Thomas and they might have to tie a rope on the calf's feet and pull it out.

I suppose few young women today would consider it a compliment to have a calf named in her honor as an engagement present, but I think my mother was pleased. Sharon View Helen became a handsome cow with a spot accenting one eye much like General Patton's bulldog.

All of our cows had names. Purebred animals had to be registered by name, pedigree, and picture. In the 1940s when photographic film was needed for the war effort, Mother had to draw the markings of each baby calf on the certificate being submitted for registration—left side, right side and full face drawn on the calf outline on the certificate. I suppose today it is all done with a digital camera and images transferred via internet. Sometimes I helped with the drawing and naming. I believe Mother liked the job of thinking up names for all of the calves—"Scotch Lassie," "Bright Token," "Heather Mist," "May Mischief."

The Ayrshire breed originated in Scotland like my Mother's ancestors and she liked names with a Scottish connection. She and Daddy were excited when the British king and queen visited the United States in 1939 because King George VI kept an Ayrshire herd at Balmoral castle and served as a patron of the Ayrshire Breeders' Association in Britain.

That was the year of the World's Fair in New York City and the

Borden Company sponsored an electrified farm exhibit where city folks could see live cows from each of the major dairy breeds being milked with DeLaval milking machines. But dairymen were distressed that the Coca Cola drinks selling at the fair for five cents a bottle was more popular than milk at ten cents a half-pint. It was the beginning of a trend they would never reverse.

To those of us who worked with them daily, each of our cows had her own personality. It was a beautiful sight to watch them in the late afternoon coming down the lane from the hillside pasture, displaying themselves in a single file led by Sharon View Mary, the dowager queen of the herd during my childhood. She was four years older than I, but seemed to get better with age. When our herd averaged 9962 pounds of milk in 1942, she produced 14027 pounds at twelve years of age—not bad for a lady approaching eighty, for each year of a cow's life equals six or seven for a human.

Mary reminded me so much of Ada the Ayrshire, the cartoon character who appeared regularly in the *Country Gentleman* magazine during those years. Ada was a wonderfully independent, fearless creature who successfully overcame every hazard around the farm. One of my favorite images was a hissing goose who confronted her in the barnyard only to find Ada nose to nose, sticking out her tongue, not one bit intimidated. Our Mary could have been Ada's model. Every cow in the herd deferred to her, but by the time I knew her she was old enough to have earned the rank.

It was years later that Carnation Milk began advertising "milk from contented" cows, but I used to think that was true of ours. Daddy's cows lived such an unusually long and productive life that he was pictured with Queen of Maples in an *Ayrshire Digest* article about university research relating bovine longevity to profit. Cows normally had their first calf at two years of age and university researchers found that it took two years in production to pay for the first four years of feed and labor costs before the farmer could begin to make a profit. A cow who ceased producing at six was profitable only two years while one who produced until the age of ten had six profitable years, making her equal to three ordinary cows. Daddy had several who were productive well into their teens, which was very old indeed for cows.

He was convinced that good food and care with a regular milking schedule was rewarded with longevity and productivity. As he approached his ninetieth birthday, I found myself wondering whether he himself was reaping the benefits he had practiced with his cattle.

When pasture was lush and daylight was long, our cows often responded like boys playing baseball with the score tied and neglected to come to the barn on time. Dave or I would be sent to round them up. Whistling for Lassie to come along, we usually stopped under the sassafras tree at the top of the lane to collect one of the mitten-shaped leaves that we licked to make them stick to our hands and give ourselves green palms.

As the cows reached the open barn door each filed obediently into her own stall, placing her head through the open metal stanchion— two upright metal bars that would be closed to fasten her in the stall for milking. Beside each stanchion was a metal bowl with a lever that the cow could press with her nose to get a drink of water, and most tested it immediately upon arrival just like a toddler passing a drinking fountain. In the manger in front of her a small mound of ground feed would be waiting for her, scooped from the wooden feed cart whose wheels squeaked as it was rolled the length of the concrete center aisle.

I took over this job from Daddy about the age of nine or ten when I knew enough math to understand fractions. Once a month Daddy would determine how many scoops each cow should receive depending on her current productivity and the season of the year. In the winter each cow received silage topped with ground corn that had been mixed with a feed supplement, but when they were on summer pasture that substituted for silage—just like summer salads for their human counterparts.

Calves were separated from their mothers when they were three days old, allowing their mother's milk to be reserved for human consumers. As early as I can remember it was my job to feed the calves. Babies had to be taught to drink milk from a bucket, and from this they were gradually weaned to "Larro Calf Starter," —which like breakfast cereal for humans kept them from getting diarrhea.

I taught them to drink by giving the calf a finger to suck and then slowly dropping my hand into the warm milk in the bottom of the bucket. Even baby calves have scratchy tongues that tickle your fingers as they suck. Because nature has programed them to encourage their mother's flow of milk by bumping her udder, you had to hold the bucket tightly between your knees or they would butt it right out of your hands and splash milk over both of you. Feeding baby calves was more like play than work, and I loved to pet their soft fuzzy heads, feeling the knobs where horns would soon grow.

When calves were a few months old, they were separated by sex and young bulls were sold to other breeders as prospective herd sires. Our registered bull calves were far too valuable to become veal for someone's dinner table. Even during the war, we had a steady stream of visiting cattle buyers. Some of the heifers were sold, too, but those with the best pedigrees were kept as replacements as less productive cows were sold or older cows failed to produce a calf and were sent to the stockyard. Sometimes one of the best bull calves would be kept as our junior sire for a couple of years, but Daddy didn't like to breed a bull to his half-sisters and only used him on the older cows.

Every three or four years Daddy would be on the lookout for the best bull calf he could buy to become his new herd sire. It was quite a gamble because a bull would be at least fifteen to eighteen months old before he could be used for breeding, then nine months before his first calves were born, two years before the heifers were bred and calved, and then nearly a year before their production was recorded and you could begin to evaluate them. It was like buying a lottery ticket and waiting nearly six years to discover whether you had a winner.

In April 1939, Daddy made national news in the *Ayshire Digest* by paying $300 (about $5500 today) to reserve an unborn calf, provided it was a bull, from an outstanding cow at Fillmore Farm, a large herd at Bennington, Vermont. Experienced breeders considered this a real gamble, but Fillmore Knickerbocker sired some excellent calves and Daddy sold him four years later to a herd in Connecticut for $2500 (about $39,000 today) one of the highest prices paid in the US for an Ayrshire herd sire to that date.

It was his offspring that caused Mother to note in her diary one day in 1943, "had bull buyers from three states today." Although Daddy and Mother were too busy to travel, the world was coming to their door—from Pinehurst, North Carolina to Oconomowoc, Wisconsin to Salem, Virginia. Of course, Daddy kept track. Years later he proudly told me that in addition to Ohio breeders he had sold cattle to twenty-one states and Columbia, South America.

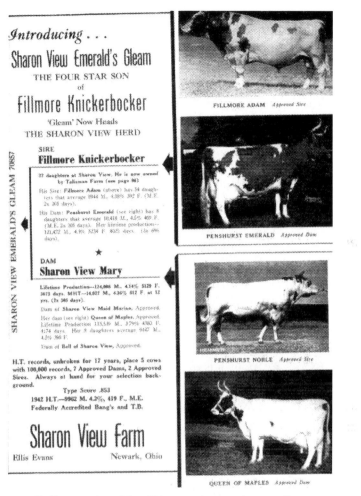

Full page Ayrshire Digest ad introducing first
home grown Sharon View Herd Sire

In 1943, Daddy decided to keep one of Knickerbacker's sons as a home-bred herd sire and introduced him to the Ayrshire community with a full page advertisement in the Ayrshire Digest. This cost $35 (about $540 today) and I'm sure was not a decision my parents made lightly. But Sharon View Emerald's Gleam had a very special pedigree being the son of Knickerbacker and our legendary Sharon View Mary. My father was making a big bet on Gleam and was willing to sell many of his sisters in order to keep him as a herd sire.

Appearance was important among registered cattle breeders. For a number of years I remember Professor Salisbury from the Ohio State University bringing his student judging team out to our farm to practice placing two or three selected groups of cows and heifers in rank order based on type characteristics. Professor Salisbury would compare rankings with Daddy before announcing the winners and team members would go on to compete in regional and national competitions.

During the war, when most state and county fairs were canceled, the Ayrshire Breeders' Association began a program to measure and improve quality by urging farmers to have their herds classified, or graded for type—a Miss America contest for cows! University professors ranked each animal on a chart that measured strength and vigor through features such as height at the shoulders, girth around the heart, width of hips, and length of rump. Of course the capacity and shape of the udder and long, branching mammary veins were an indication of productivity. A score of 90% or better rated excellent, and dropped by increments from very good, to good plus, to good, to fair. Every cow in the herd had to be included and any cow rating less than 70% would have her registration canceled. No bull calves could be registered from any cow classifying less than 75%. That first year Sharon View cows averaged a "very good" 86.7%.

At the time, the national association had more than 5000 member herds and the classification system actually gave visibility to small high-quality herds like Sharon View which could not afford the advertising of larger ones. The next year the association launched a Constructive Breeder Award, recognizing five herds the first year for having at least 65% of their cows bred and raised on the farm, a herd classification average of 82.5% or better, and a production average of at least 9250 pounds of milk at 3.9% butterfat on twice a day milking. My father exceeded those goals every year, winning a succession of certificates that I'm sure he treasured as much as any actor with an Academy Award Oscar.

Years later I leafed through a stack of *Ayrshire Digest* magazines from the war years, proud of the occasional half-page advertisement for Sharon View Farm. Often they feature photos of our cows—Martha, Ivy, Ada, Belle—taken with Mother's box camera in the pasture field. I smile at the contrast with the advertisements from large herds featuring professionally posed animals just out of the show ring. I don't have to wonder where I learned to do my best and stand by it proudly. Year after year my father's herd of about twenty cows bred on the farm competed quite favorably with larger herds that had been acquired at far higher cost.

I have no idea what my parents' income was during my childhood. That was something we simply did not discuss. Most of it naturally came from the sale of dairy products, but when surplus animals were offered for sale they did well. In the 1944 spring sale of the Ohio Ayrshire Breeders, Sharon View Lass of Dreams topped the sale at $425—when all cows averaged $290—and the first daughter of Fillmore Knickerbocker was the highest priced heifer calf at $255, when the average was $139.

Trying my best, I can't remember if we were given an allowance for doing daily chores. But I must have had something by the time I started school for I distinctly remember taking a dime each week to put in the slot in the cardboard folder we kids kept until we had enough to buy a war bond. And I also had a dime for the Sunday school collection every week. When I turned ten I was old enough to join the Licking County 4-H Dairy Club. Daddy gave me a heifer calf to raise each year. He paid for her food and I took care of her and trained her to show at the local Hartford Fair. I kept any prize money I won by putting it into a bank account toward my college education and my heifer grew into a member of my father's herd.

There was an emotional bond between my father and his Ayrshires that I never shared. By the time I graduated from the eighth grade, I resented the cows and their domination of our lives. I had resolved that I was going to college and I would never marry a farmer!

7

$$\cdots\!\!\cdot\!\!\blacklozenge\!\!\cdot\!\!\cdots$$

All Creatures Great and Small

Horses were the most valuable animals on the farm during my father's childhood, but my earliest memories during the late 1930s are during the transition from draft horses to tractors. I can remember our team pulling the wagon as my father or the hired man stacked it with hay, and proudly being allowed to hold the reins to drive. But I realize now this was a routine that men and horses had down pat, and that it was a "Giddy'up" from Daddy or Willis, busy stacking hay onto the wagon, rather than the reins in my childish hands that told the team when to step forward.

They must have been tame beasts because I can remember riding on the back of one when my father led them to the barn where they were kept up the road. This was usually Willis' job on his way home, but I remember the rare and special times when I walked home afterwards with my busy father.

For some time after my father got his first tractor—a red Farmall A with sixteen to eighteen horsepower that seems puny by modern standards but powerful compared to a team of real horses. We still had

Art---a broad-backed mix between draft horse and pony---perhaps as an insurance policy in case the tractor had to be pulled from the mud, but I remember him as mine to ride bareback.

Art and my job during hay making was to pull rope to the fork that dumped the hay into the mow. When a wagon of hay was pulled into the barn, Willis would pull down the grapple fork that operated with pulleys and ran along a rail that lined the barn roof above the hay mows. When he had pulled the huge prongs apart and set them firmly into the load of hay, he would give me a shout and I would give Art a kick of the heels that would start him across the farmyard toward the garden fence. Art knew as well as I exactly how far to go depending on whether we were dumping hay into the first, second, or third mow, and I could feel the weight release when Willis pulled the trip rope to drop the hay. It wasn't nearly as much fun in later years when I did the same job with the tractor.

Actually I learned to ride on Dixie, a fat black pony who retired to our farm after years of service in a commercial pony ride that carried youngsters around in circles at county fairs. Like any assembly-line worker, Dixie had long ago mastered the art of performing the necessities but no more. The minute you approached with a saddle she knew to take a deep breath and blow her belly large to avoid being tightly cinched, so you jiggled the cinch and waited until she thought you were through and re-tightened the girths.

I saw Dixie as my ticket to the farthest reaches of our farm, or our entire neighborhood. By kicking my heels and shaking the reins she could be induced to start out—at the slowly measured walk of a commercial pony ride. Only by shouts accompanied by slapping reins and kicking heels could I persuade her to trot a few steps. Dixie mostly walked.

We both enjoyed the shady ride that the trees provided along our creek, but Dixie would really have preferred to be rider less and delighted in ducking under low hanging branches that might scrape me off.

The minute I turned her around to head home toward the barn, she became a race horse with a canter that belied her age and overweight condition. Art had the same habit, but since we had no saddle to fit his broad back I always rode him bareback. One afternoon someone had left a load of hay in his usual path to the barn, and as he came to an abrupt halt I went sailing over his head onto the hay much to the surprise of us both.

Despite their faults I loved Dixie and Art. For years I sketched horses and dreamed of living on a ranch in Wyoming. The affections of either horse were easily won with a carrot grubbed from the garden or a handful of oats from the bin. I marveled at the velvety softness of their noses and the delicacy with which they nibbled from my fingers. Art was ten times the size of a baby calf but his satiny nostrils were a dramatic contrast to the calf's firm nose and raspy tongue. I was convinced that horses were superior beings and if I were to return to earth in a second incarnation I prayed to come back as a horse.

The smartest animal on our farm—except for humans, and sometimes that was a close call—was Lassie. Unlike her famous namesake who left me weeping over the misfortunes she encountered in *Lassie Come Home*, our Lassie had no golden mane like a lion. She was a purebred border collie, and I have no idea why my parents decided she would be a desirable addition to a farm that had no sheep. Perhaps they thought those inbred skills would translate to cows. She was smaller than her famous namesake, with long black hair except for a small triangle of white like a cowboy's handkerchief tied beneath her neck. Her most distinguishing characteristic was a pair of big brown eyes that watched every move you made and instantly read your intentions.

Lassie was a cuddly puppy just recently weaned when she arrived on our farm. Finally Dave and I had a pet of our own, or so we thought.

She knew better. Without a mother or a human to guide her, she became a bouncy puppy running semicircles back and forth across the farmyard collecting Mother's black hens into a neat cluster. It was a procedure that rivaled comic opera. From birth these chickens had enjoyed free range, pecking their way among choice tidbits of grain dropped from wagons or between garden rows abundantly strewn with ripe vegetable droppings. They vigorously protested this black shadow that insisted they seek their nourishment in unison, flapping their wings at this troublesome creature in a contest of wills that Lassie always won.

From her mastery of hens, Lassie found it a small step to dairy cows who were many times her size but more accustomed to the demands of human authority. She was soon saving Dave and me many a chase in rounding up the stray cow who wandered through a broken fence into lush grass and saw little need to respond to our "Soo, bossy. Soo, bossy." When it came to frisky yearling heifers being moved from one pasture to another Lassie was pure genius, anticipating their breakaway thoughts before their leg muscles could respond with more than a step or two.

Lassie slept in the barn. She was a working dog and every other animal on the farm soon understood that she was in charge. As a teenager beginning to consider the possible directions my life might take, I remember sitting with my arm draped across Lassie rubbing her ear lightly as her eyes searched my thoughts. She had no answer for my questions, for her destiny was bred in her genes and I simply marveled that it could be so.

Cats were pretty much low man on the totem pole on our farm. They lived in the barn and their job was to control the population of mice that were attracted to the granary, but we usually supplemented their diet with a saucer of milk at milking time. There were usually five or six, meowing and running between your legs, anxious to get their share. Most were quite tame and would purr like a motor when Dave and I petted them, but Mother would never let us bring a cat into the house. Cats were not pets and ours were never given names.

Cats were expendable. Young tomcats usually ran away and old tabbies disappeared to die, but it was no great loss in an environment that would soon produce another litter of kittens. We rarely saw the tomcats that roamed the neighborhood, but sometimes in the night you could hear them howling or fighting. Daddy said tomcats were defending their territory like wildcats.

I don't think our tabbies had much trouble giving birth. They usually had litters of three or four kittens at a time and often we never even knew until we found their nest in the haymow or behind some feed sacks. Compared to newborn calves who would be standing up within a few minutes, baby kittens were blind helpless creatures who didn't even open their eyes for a couple of weeks. Often we wouldn't discover them until their mother decided it was time to move them from their birth nest to a more convenient place and we would see her carrying one by the scruff of its neck, its body swinging carelessly from side to side as she walked. It was fun to watch her go back and forth, making a separate trip for each one. Baby kittens seemed to trust their mother implicitly and never made a sound or struggled to get free.

8

Hollyhock Dolls and Secret Places

Like a bird watcher training his binoculars on the treetops, when I focus on childhood memories I discover vivid images flashing into view—a skinny little girl of about five or six with hollyhock dolls lined up in parade formation on the large stone step leading to the back porch outside our kitchen.

Hollyhocks grew from seed dropped the previous year along the back of our house, quickly growing higher than my head and offering an abundance of blossoms from palest pink to magenta. I think it was Cousin Gwen who taught me how to create a doll by inserting the stem of a fully opened blossom into the bud of another to create a head and a body wearing a circular skirt. I can still feel the chill of the mossy stone step against my bare legs as I carefully executed the process, talking as I worked, telling each doll about the ball that she was about to attend. How I loved their swirling pink skirts as I lined them up in dance formation—a configuration that years later I would recognize with a smile was remarkably similar to the whirling dervishes of Mevlevi. How apt. My hollyhock dolls allowed me to escape into a fantasy world, but a world more glamorous than spiritual. A world where I, of course, was the graceful star receiving the curtsies of my subjects

I did have a real doll baby—one with a rubberized face that you could wipe clean, hair that had been crimped into a curl, and arms and legs that you could move. I don't know why I rarely played with her, but I can't remember her being very interesting. What fascinated me for hours were paper dolls.

Paper dolls were my generation's Barbie. They had sophisticated adult figures with curvaceous bosoms and legs. Each was perforated so you could punch her out of the book, and so were all of the clothes and accessories on the following pages. Each blouse, skirt, hat or pair of shoes had tabs that could be folded back to hold them in place as you dressed your doll. What fun to mix and match outfits endlessly.

Paper dolls were sociable companions for a solitary little girl who consulted them endlessly about whether they liked the white or the blue sweater with the plaid skirt, and would she rather wear the black flats or the brown sandals. But many of their clothes were party dresses of sleek satin and sequins and I had no more knowledge of a glamorous world where people attended concerts and the theater than my inanimate paper dolls.

Unlike the hollyhock dolls who had an exciting life during the few hours before they wilted, paper dolls lived with me day in and day out, faithful companions to my every whim. Some of the books even had paper doll families — father, mother, brother and sister. Families usually came with two parents and two children, just like ours. I had no idea that I was being acculturated to the middle-class American ideal nuclear family of the 1940s.

But best of all were my secret places. Hiding places. Like the nests in the haymow where you could curl up with two or three kittens, their eyes newly open and just learning to walk, purring like buzzing bees if you stoked their fur.

As soon as I learned to read, a book usually joined me in my hideout under the wisteria bush at the front porch. It stretched for eight or ten feet with leafy tendrils offering perfect concealment while letting in sufficient sunshine for reading. Here I spent hours on the mountain with Heidi or by the seashore with Anne of Green Gables. How I dreamed of snow-covered peaks and endless ocean waves. Reading Little Women I wished that I had sisters to share adventures with like Jo March. It was always tomboy Jo that I identified with.

About the time we got our pony Dixie I became totally engrossed in horses, reading *Black Beauty, My Friend Flicka, and Thunderhead*—sketching horses' heads with flying manes on any scrap of paper, dreaming of galloping across the prairies when I was grown up and could live on a ranch in Wyoming. I was about thirty before I finally achieved that gallop across an open prairie, and paid for it with days of sore thighs that had long forgotten how to grip the muscular back of a horse.

To this day I'm not sure what is so fascinating to children about hiding places—a sense of security or having someplace special that can't be shared by adults. We had them inside the house, too. Once when I was very small I hid between the living room piano and fireplace—I can't remember why unless it was to escape from my brother.

Eventually Mother and Daddy realized that neither one had seen me for some time and recalled that they had seen a car of gypsies — a common term at the time for homeless people — pass by on the road. Their frantic calls while searching convinced me that I must have done something terribly wrong, and I quietly made myself as invisible as possible. I was surprised when Mother discovered me to be hugged rather than spanked, but my childhood world gave me a freedom to roam that would shock any modern parent haunted by images of child molesters.

When we were small, mother would drape a blanket over our round dining room table and allow us to take pots and pans from the kitchen cupboard into our playhouse. And one of my favorite reading places was lying flat on my stomach under mother's upright piano. It helped me feel protected while my imagination journeyed into the wondrous worlds of medieval courts and foreign lands where people dressed in strange costumes.

The bed in my room was an antique four-poster that had been in mother's family for generations, and I begged and begged for a canopy like the ones I had seen pictured in books. We hunted for one that mother could make, finally finding a picture of the perfect white eyelet canopy with ruffles all around. Just dreaming about it made me feel like a queen. I'm sure mother really intended to make it for me, but it became one of the many things that, as a busy farm wife, she never got around to doing. As an adult I understand her demanding schedule, but as a child it was a huge disappointment. By the time I was a teenager and could have made it myself, I preferred striped wallpaper and pictures of horses to white eyelet ruffles. Perhaps I had outgrown my need for secret places.

Mother often, however, found time to read to us before bedtime, a very special sharing time that made books seem magic. And a real treat of treats was an afternoon thunderstorm that darkened the sky and sent flashes of lightening followed by crashes of thunder. Mother immediately stopped her work to gather Dave and me. All three of us would lie on our stomachs on the living room carpet while she read a story, safely cocooned from the violence outside. To this day I have a fondness for storms that traces to those rare moments.

But Mother also knew there were times when children liked to be scared. A favorite game would have her sitting sternly cross-legged on the floor with arms folded Buddha style, intoning in her deepest voice, "I—am—a statue—made—of—stone! I—cannot— move!" Laughing and screaming we would circle her cautiously, trying to pry loose a rigid finger or hand, knowing that after some moments the statue would spring to life and grab one of us in its arms. The other would dash for the safety of Daddy's lap, and he would protest that we were getting too excited before bedtime. But we loved every minute and begged for more. The scary movies of Dracula and King Kong were never in our budget, but we had the same effect in our living room with mother's "Statue Made of Stone."

Except for my brother, my early childhood lacked playmates and I realize I missed learning the socialization skills that are an important focus of modern pre-schools. But there were abundant opportunities for exercising our creativity—a tradeoff perhaps, even though many town children had both.

9

Hand-me-down Shoes and Lemon Meringue Pie

We weren't poor. We just didn't have money. But few of the people we knew had much money in the Depression and during the war there was so little gasoline to go shopping and such a shortage of consumer goods, it didn't really matter. I had never known it any other way.

Although I never tasted a hamburger sandwich with French fries until I was an adult, hunger was impossible with our bountiful garden and ready milk supply. We relished a simple Sunday night supper of bread and milk or mush fried in butter and topped with maple syrup. Mother made mush by cooking cornmeal in water until it was thick, poured it into a loaf pan to chill and harden, and then sliced it for frying. It was delicious smothered in the maple syrup we got from a neighbor.

But we were less thrilled with the endless mounds of cottage cheese. During vacations at Denison University, our milk supply exceeded the demand of our family and retail customers. Mother set the milk on the back porch until it turned sour and then poured it through a cheesecloth stretched tight over a large kettle to save the curd and allow the liquid whey to drain off. When it stopped dripping, she gathered up the cloth and squeezed it as tightly as possible to remove the sour-tasting whey, but the "pot cheese" of my childhood was a crumbly, sour product that we children smothered with honey or apple butter to mask its flavor.

Much of our protein came from the eggs of the hens that roamed throughout the barnyard. Descended from Black Jersey Giants that my mother prized as large roasting fowl, these hens lived in a chicken coop that was lined on three sides with wooden nesting boxes. I hated, absolutely hated, gathering eggs. This was a task that forced you to enter the foul smelling chicken coop packed with layers of manure that was cleaned out once a year and made excellent fertilizer for the garden.

Trying to hold my nose with my left hand without spilling eggs from the bucket on my arm, I would reach gingerly into each nesting box for eggs, often having to reach beneath a nesting hen who would peck my hand or fly out with a flurry that would cause me to drop the bucket. To this day, I have a terrible fear of birds flying anywhere near my face. I was so genuinely terrorized that I convinced my brother at an early age that this was a manly challenge he could handle better than I.

Sometimes we had extra eggs that mother traded at the grocery store. These were washed free of any manure and packed into cardboard egg cartons. That was how I learned that rotten eggs float in water, a very useful piece of information if one needed to get even with a brother for some piece of mischief.

I was far too squeamish to watch when it became time to catch a hen who had passed her laying prime and convert her into roasted or fried chicken for Sunday dinner. That was Mother's job, and even yet I cannot understand how she had the courage to take a hatchet and chop off its head.

I was, however, drafted to help with the next stage. Mother would prepare a teakettle of boiling water which she poured over the dead bird to loosen its feathers—creating an acrid smell of singed feathers that those who have experienced it can never forget. Mother usually plucked the large outer feathers by the hand full, leaving me the task of pulling the pin feathers. Few things are more repulsive than the wrinkled yellow skin of a dead chicken spotted with black pin feathers that must be pulled out one at a time from disgusting places such as crevices under the wings.

Despite my participation in this trauma, I loved fried chicken—rolled in flour, fried in lard in a big black iron skillet. Our Sunday dinners were undoubtedly as bad for our arteries as they were good for our soul. Daddy and Grandma each got one side of the breast, Dave and I the drumsticks, Mother the heart, liver, and back. Mother was such a good actress I really thought she preferred the back until after Grandma died and I realized that she had been sacrificing to let everyone else have the choice pieces.

Others may praise the dishwasher or the microwave oven as the inventions which have liberated the modern homemaker—and I, too, appreciate their wonder—but for me they pale in significance beside the convenience of going to a supermarket and purchasing skinless, boneless chicken breasts or thighs in a shrink-wrapped package. I know very well where my food comes from, but I would not be able to perform the murder personally.

Not everything we ate was home grown, of course. Mother regularly bought supplies at Fuller's Market in Granville, a lovely store with an oiled wooden floor whose aroma mingled with various spices. Item by item Mr. Fuller would assemble mother's order on the linoleum counter top, using a pole with grasping hooks to reach a box of Kellogg's cornflakes high on a shelf behind him. Mother bought staples like sugar and flour, but very rarely tea or coffee—only if company was expected. Milk was our beverage. In the winter she sometimes bought bananas or Florida oranges as a treat. We invariably found a tangerine, a very special treat, in the toe of our Christmas stocking.

Meat usually came from the rented freezer locker in Newark that my folks filled by purchasing half a hog from a butchering neighbor that was cut into pork chops and ground into sausage, and a quarter of beef that was cut into pot roasts to be cooked with potatoes, onions, and carrots. If Mother bought meat from Mr. Fuller's butcher case, it was usually a slice of beef round that he cut and wrapped in white butcher's paper and tied with string from the ball that hung above his scale. Mother would cut this into pieces that were dipped in flour and browned like fried chicken, then simmered until they were tender and had formed their own gravy for mashed potatoes.

Many times Mother would have other errands to run at the hardware store or the drugstore and she would drop me off at the library. The Granville Library was—and still is with a modern addition to the rear—a warm golden sandstone that managed to be both welcoming and impressive as you climbed its front steps and entered through a massive oak door. In my day, you immediately faced the circular librarian's desk where a stern-faced lady accepted any books I was returning and eyed me over her reading glasses as I quietly made my way into the children's area on the right. Low tables with small chairs were inviting, but I much preferred the window seats in the two high arched windows that overlooked Broadway—what an impressive name the optimistic founders had given the main street of their village plat. Here I could curl up and read but still watch for Mother coming to pick me up.

Dave and I were convinced that we could run faster in new shoes, and we celebrated by chasing each other round and around the dining room table. New shoes were a tradition every spring and fall in the years when we were about four to eight and our feet were growing like Labrador puppies. I would get a brand new pair of brown oxfords and

Dave would inherit my old ones—new to him as only a younger child can appreciate.

Buying new shoes was an adventure that involved climbing onto the X-ray machine with a viewer on top that let Mother and the salesman compare the bones of our feet to the edge of the shoe and measure the space available for growth. I couldn't see through the viewer without a boost from the sales clerk but he was always obliging and lifted me to inspect Dave's feet and then give him a turn to view mine. We thought it was hilarious to see our feet like a skeleton of bones.

Mother made most of our clothes through grade school, but every fall before school started we would go shopping for new underwear and socks. Newark had two real department stores---Carroll's and King's. Carroll's main attraction was the elevator, the only one in town. It was run by an elderly man who sat on a stool by the door to shut the folding screen and doors. Then, holding the brass knob, he moved the handle to number two or three for the upper floors. Sometimes we arrived with a bump and he had to jostle the handle a time or two to align the elevator with the floor before opening the door.

King's was fascinating in a different way, for the interior was an open oval like a doughnut with a second story balcony all the way around that customers reached by climbing stairs. Pneumatic tubes— like the ones used today at bank drive-through windows—stretched from sales counters on each floor all the way up and around the store to a windowed office in one corner of the second floor, carrying the sales slip and the customer's money, returning with a whoosh to deliver the receipt and change. The tubes were clear plastic and we loved to watch the entire journey, never dreaming that we would live to see credit and debit cards replace real money.

I must have been eleven—the first year after the war and the abolition of gas rationing—when Mother and I first went to Columbus to shop. I think the occasion was to buy each of us a new dress to attend an Ayrshire banquet at the Deshler Hotel—the capital city's tallest and finest—where Daddy was going to receive an award.

This was my first "store bought" dress and it was packed in Mother's cedar chest long after I outgrew it. It was an A-line aqua crepe—of a shade that I would later see in the shallow waters off the Bermuda shore—decorated with a spray of peach colored flowers appliqued across the bodice. I felt as special and as grown up in that dress as any I have ever owned.

From then until I graduated from high school, Columbus shopping trips for school clothes became a treasured annual event. Mother and I usually ended up in the fabric department on the fifth floor of Lazarus, the largest department store in Columbus. Here bolts and bolts of cottons, silks, and woolens tempted us like the wonders of an Arabian bazaar. By then I had learned that if I sewed them myself I could have three new outfits for the price of one.

We usually checked out several other stores along High St., but the highlight of the day was lunch at Mills cafeteria across from the Ohio Capitol. I wonder now why we never crossed the street and explored that magnificent building, but I'm sure we never did. Was my mother intimidated or, more likely was it simply a working office building that in those days did not encourage citizen tours?

Perhaps we were anxious for the treat of eating a meal neither of us had prepared. Mills offered what seemed to us an endless array of salads, entrees, and desserts—each on its own plate or dish! Like rubes from the country, we each filled our trays with different choices, and when we reached a table immediately divided everything in half so that we could double our pleasure. One of us always had to choose lemon meringue pie and the other banana cream piled high with a fragile layer of meringue that Mother sliced slowly and carefully into two equal pieces. I can imagine the reaction of a modern teen to such unsophisticated behavior at the mall—with one's mother of all people!

10

Take Your Daughter to Work

On a family farm every day is *Take Your Daughter to Work Day*. Sharon View Dairy operated seven days a week, fifty-two weeks a year, no vacations, and no matter where you are going or what you are doing, get home in time to do the milking. Tedious as that might be, I never had to wonder what my father was doing in some remote corporate office.

Cows must be milked every morning and evening or they will quit producing. Milking was one of my father's jobs, usually with the hired man. For much of my childhood, our hired man was Willis Gatten whose family lived in a house at the back of our farm that you reached by a long lane that ran from the road past the churchyard and the entire west side of our farm. Willis was dependable and had a calm manner that was highly desirable around milk cows. Even more important, was the fact that he was a Seventh Day Adventist who regularly attended church on Saturday. He and my father worked out a system so Daddy would do the milking alone on Saturday evening and Willis alone on Sunday, leaving each of them a day of leisure as soon as the morning chores were done.

The R.E.A. (Rural Electrification Administration) had reached Sharon Valley by the time I was old enough to be around the barn during milking, and DeLaval "Magnetic Milking Machines" had replaced the tedious process of milking each cow by hand. DeLaval regularly advertised in the Ayrshire Digest and during the war was one of many manufacturing companies that cut their own production to proudly make critical parts for the government.

DeLaval WWII ad in Ayrshire Digest

Daddy knew how to do every job that had to be done on the dairy farm and had taught Willis, and Al Smith, the man who did the pasteurizing and bottling in the milk room, how to do each job the way he expected.

I loved to watch Daddy attach the cucumber-shaped suction cups to a cow's udder. He always stepped on the right hand side so the cow wouldn't be startled, grabbed her tail with his left hand so she wouldn't swat him in the face, and leaned his forehead against her flank while he first carefully washed her udder with warm water and coaxed a stream of milk from each teat.

I loved to watch. "Why do you do that?'

"That's so she will know it is time to let her milk down."

How well I remember the day he glanced up and saw me watching intently. "Do you want to try it?" Of course I did.

"Step right here. I'll hold her tail for you."

I stepped in and stroked her flank before I bent down and took hold of a front teat the way I had seen him do it. But when I pulled nothing happened.

"Keep trying. She knows you're nervous. Just pretend you are pulling a rope."

Sure enough, a stream of milk squirted right onto my foot, but I looked up and knew from his face that I shouldn't squeal with delight. He just said matter-of-factly, "Now do the other teats just like that."

"Hey, I'm milking!" When I had started all four I gave her flank an appreciative pat and stepped back to let my father attach the cups. He set the machine in the stall and attached it to the line that ran above the stanchions that held the cow's head and kept her in the stall, flared the suction cups in his left hand like open flower petals, and then quickly attached one to each teat.

One time he placed a cup on my finger so I would know how it felt—just like a baby calf when I gave it a finger to suck while I maneuvered it in or out of its pen.

Sometimes I would stand and watch the milk flowing through the clear tubing into the pail of the milking machine, at first so fast that it was completely white and later in spurts that meant it was almost done.

R.E.A. was wonderful. But it ran for miles along rural roads thick with trees. If we had a thunderstorm—or an ice storm in winter—it was almost certain that a tree or branches would fall across the electric lines at some point. Everyone in the neighborhood counted on Mother to call and let the company know when the electricity went out, for our milking machines, walk-in cooler, and dairy bottling equipment depended on it. On the rare occasions when repair crews couldn't fix the problem in a few hours, Mother would have to pitch in and help Daddy and Willis—and by the time we were teenagers Dave and I as well—in the tedious job of milking by hand. If you skipped a milking, it would only be a day or two before the cows would begin to go dry.

Many years later, recalling how my parents depended on the R.E.A., I wondered why, as staunch Republicans, they blasted President Roosevelt and his New Deal policies. But by then I had learned that political opinions were rarely rational and sometimes it is best simply to agree to disagree.

In the dairy, Al Smith reigned supreme in high rubber boots—a mirage amid the steam rising from the vats where glass milk bottles were scrubbed with a brush and sterilized with steam. All the while he would be keeping an eye on the temperature gauge above the huge aluminum vat filled with milk. Sharon View Dairy was one of the first in the area to offer pasteurized rather that raw milk and Al watched closely to see that the milk reached the critical stage of 142 but no more than 145 degrees and held there for thirty minutes. Any less and it wouldn't be safe from bacteria, any longer and it would be scalded and taste funny.

It was the next stage that I most liked to watch, when he released the hot milk to flow like a rippling waterfall over a series of pipes filled with cold spring water, and into a small vat protected from flies by a cheese cloth cover. From here a spout poured it into the sterilized glass bottles that rotated into position on a turntable and were sealed when he pulled a lever that released a cardboard cap and pressed it tightly into the neck of each quart bottle. Full bottles were placed into crates that held a dozen and could be stacked four or five tiers high in the big walk-in cooler.

This bottling process happened three days a week to be ready for delivery on the retail route in Granville early the next morning. On

Ellis at bottling machine   Ellis at feed cart in barn

alternate days the pasteurized milk flowed into aluminum five-gallon cans—the kind you occasionally see today in antique shops decoratively painted with flowers. These were delivered to the Denison University dormitories to fill large pitchers for each table. Those were the days when college students sat down in a dining room and were served their meals rather than going through a cafeteria line and picking up a cardboard carton of milk with a straw. On a hot summer day, Dave and I loved to sneak into the walk-in cooler among the aluminum cans and crates of bottles for a breathtaking cool down that returned us shivering to the afternoon's heat.

A small room between the milk house and the barn held a concrete watering trough filled with cold water. It was here that aluminum cans filled with warm milk from the milking machines were placed to chill before being placed in the cooler. The milk house was a complicated place with a drilled well to provide an adequate cold water supply and its own coal-fired boiler to heat water and produce the steam for the sterilization and pasteurization processes. Once the cans or bottles were filled and stored in the cooler, all of the equipment had to be steam cleaned and the floor hosed down in preparation for the next day. Daddy knew the entire procedure and could do it in an emergency if Al was sick, but it was an operation that took all morning and that was when he normally delivered milk to Granville.

I didn't realize until years later when I began my teaching career, that my father knew so much and taught so many--both hired men, my brother and me, teenagers who worked part time during haymaking and threshing, and Professor Salisbury's visiting dairy judging teams. It was informal learning by doing, but it required mastering both skills and a work ethic.

When my father was at Ohio State University participating in that winter short course after high school, he became not only convinced that the dairy business offered the best farming option for the future, he became equally convinced that Ayshires were the hardiest dairy breed. That opinion was reinforced in 1929 when the Ayrshire Breeders' Association walked two Ayrshire cows, Tomboy and Alice, from their headquarters in Brandon, Vermont to the National Dairy Show in St. Louis, Missouri just to prove the breed's hardiness. Daddy proudly claimed they not only survived the walk, but calved normally, and produced well the year after. Farmers like my father wanted advertising that showed rather than told. Like most farmers, my father admired hardiness and from an early age I tried to measure up and earn his approval.

As he began to acquire Ayrshires, he first sold his milk to a creamery in Newark. When the Depression began squeezing profits, he decided to eliminate the middle man and go into the dairy business himself, hiring help with the regular farm work. Much later, when I studied about the Great Depression and read about men forced to sell apples on the streets of some cities, I asked Daddy how he found the courage to expand when jobs were disappearing all around him. He seemed surprised by the question, for he simply felt he had to work harder and earn more money.

When you have a small business—and even in the 1930s a herd of fifteen to twenty cows was small for a total dairy operation—you search for an angle to be competitive. Sharon View Dairy aimed for quality, emphasizing the unique characteristic of Ayrshire cows to produce the most naturally homogenized milk with the best protein to fat ratio of any dairy breed. No one had yet perfected a method of emulsifying fat particles so they would be evenly distributed throughout a bottle of milk and customers were used to seeing a band of yellow cream which rose to the necks of their bottles of Jersey or Guernsey milk.

My parents cooperated with researchers at Ohio State University who, working with other universities determined that naturally homogenized Ayrshire milk had the softest curd and was the most easily digested by babies and young children. The Ayrshire Breeders' Association drafted advertisements and my parents printed flyers they distributed door to door in Granville touting Ayrshire milk as the best for babies. Sharon View quickly began attracting customers and Mother assumed the responsibility for preparing monthly bills and recording payments in the account ledger.

We weren't supposed to bother Mother when she was working at the antique desk in the living room with a slant top that folded down unto wooden bars that pulled from slots on either side. This provided a writing surface and revealed four drawers with cubbyholes above them where she stuffed papers of various kinds.

Her office equipment consisted of a ten-key adding machine operated by pulling the lever after each entry, a metal filing cabinet, and a supply of pencils in one of the desk drawers sharpened with a hand cranked pencil sharpener. I was particularly fascinated by the Royal typewriter that sat on its own small wheeled metal stand because mother could type letters without looking at her fingers. How I wanted to learn to do that, and when I reached high school I finally did. It was much later before I realized that in a day when official census takers considered my mother an unemployed homemaker—or as everyone said, just a housewife—she managed the entire advertising and accounting departments of Sharon View Farm.

Ellis and Helen at Sharon View 'office' desk

Delivering the milk route was Daddy's morning job after he finished milking. Al would help him stack crates of bottles floor to ceiling—or cans if this was a delivery day for Denison—into the paneled delivery truck. By the time we were six or seven, Dave or I would go along during the summer to help so he could get home quicker and begin jobs like mowing hay or cutting wheat.

Helping with the milk route meant loading the right number of bottles—most customers had a regular order—into a metal carrier that held up to six quarts at a time to carry to the customer's door. Some people had a box with a lid on their porch where we were to put them, but many wanted us to open the kitchen door and put them in the refrigerator if no one was home. Most people in Granville, like us on the farm, never locked the doors of their house during the day.

Some of our customers had dogs that Dave and I dreaded, particularly a yippy little terrier that chased us. One day when Dave was perhaps seven or eight he started for that house with several bottles in the carrier and the barking dog ran toward him. Dave turned and started running back to the truck with the dog in hot pursuit. Suddenly he stopped, turned, and yelled "Now I am mad!" and chased the dog back, with its tail between its legs, to hide underneath the porch. It was a valuable lesson in learning to face and solve problems. "Now I am mad!" became a family code—a warning Dave and I both understood meant we had reached our limit and whoever was teasing the other had to stop. Our parents didn't have time to solve sibling squabbles.

If Daddy was delivering to Denison University, he had to lift the five-gallon cans—which weighted sixty or seventy pounds when full— from the truck and roll them into the cooler in each of the three kitchens that served a dormitory complex. He always checked to be sure that the fresh cans were arranged at the back of the cooler and any leftovers were put near the front before bringing the empty cans back to the truck. There wasn't anything Dave and I could do to help here, but if the cooks were baking and we were lucky enough to find cookies just out of the oven we might be offered a sample.

Other people came and went in the work of the farm. One of the most interesting was Frank Morrow, our milk tester. Sharon View was on the DHIR (Dairy Herd Improvement Record) program that meant each month a technician came to our farm and collected milk samples from each cow at the evening and next morning milking to test the butterfat content. It was supposed to be a surprise so you couldn't skip a milking to boost your production average. A farmer wasn't to know the tester was coming until he drove in, but my father could usually guess within a span of several days.

Frank slept in our spare bedroom and Mother could be counted on for a good supper that night. I suppose it was a bit of a nuisance for Daddy and Willis to have him collect samples from each cow before they dumped the milking machine, but I loved to watch Frank work in the little room where Al washed the milk cans.

He looked a bit like the scarecrow Mother made for the garden with a plaid shirt and flapping denim legs, for Frank always wore coveralls that were splattered with holes from the hydrochloric acid he used in his tests. He sat his round centrifuge about the size of a bushel basket on the counter by the electric outlet, and when he lifted the domed lid you could see the racks with round holes to hold the glass tubes of milk he collected. I had to stand back while he poured a little acid from a glass bottle into each tube of milk. Then he plugged the machine in and let it spin. When it was done he used something that looked like tweezers to measure the golden band of fat at the top of each tube.

"What's that?" I wanted to know.

"It's called a caliper. Do you see how I can move the arms to measure the width of the fat band?"

Yes, I could see the sharp points that marked the line. Frank was nice. He never seemed to mind if I stuck my nose close as he raised each tube to the light to measure exactly. Sometimes he even let me write the numbers in the ledger he kept.

Daddy paid close attention to these records, expecting all but the two-year-old cows to produce 10,000 or more pounds of milk with 3.9 percent butterfat during the 305 day testing year. Then cows were allowed to go dry and rest for a couple of months before calving. That meant that over the course of a year each of our cows filled about 6,000 of those quart bottles we carried to customers.

The nastiest job on the farm by far was cleaning manure from the barn each morning and this fell to Willis while Daddy delivered the milk route. During the winter, straw was spread in each cow's stall for her to lie on overnight and every morning when the cows were turned out to drink and exercise, soiled patches were removed with a three-tined pitchfork and the gutter that ran behind the stalls was scooped clean of manure with a shovel. The manure was carted by a wheelbarrow to a pile in the barnyard that grew larger as the winter progressed.

By early March—when the ground was still frozen and not muddy—manure was forked from the pile into a spreader that looked like a wagon with sides and had an auger on the back that tossed clods of manure on the stubble as it ran across last year's hay field. We produced our own fertilizer from animal waste and spread it on the field before plowing for this year's corn crop. The second phase of Willis's morning chores was much more pleasant, for he shook out fresh straw, filled the manger with hay, and refilled the feed-cart from the silo and granary.

Spring through fall, of course, was the busiest time on the farm. Beginning in late March or early April when Daddy and Willis started to plow ground to plant corn, until November when the husked corn was stored in the crib, there was a variety of work to be done—mostly by Daddy and Willis, but sometimes with Uncle Doc, or with extra help hired for making hay and husking corn, and always the crew for threshing wheat.

My first memories coincide almost precisely with my father's transition from horse to tractor power. Although the first tractor was invented in 1902 and large machines with gang plows began to work the western prairies within a few years, small mid-western farmers like my father skipped the phase of heavy metal wheeled tractors, keeping their trusty teams until farm implement manufacturers perfected a smaller all-purpose tractor.

International Harvester—the descendant of the company spawned by Cyrus McCormick's famous reaper—was the first to mass produce an effective row-crop tractor. This machine was tall and narrow to clear growing corn and give the driver visibility for cultivating. Its most obvious difference was its tricycle design with two small front wheels that drove between corn rows and allowed the operator to turn a tight circle at the end of a row. With the advent of rubber tires in the 1930s, the operator had a more comfortable ride and the fact that they offered less resistance than the old cog wheels meant farmers used less fuel and were able to use a higher gear and work faster.

My father's first tractor was a Farmall A that International Harvester introduced in 1939, a bright red tricycle model with a four-cylinder engine that delivered sixteen to eighteen horsepower. I think Daddy bought his a year later, but kept his team of horses for a few years, alternating jobs and probably assuring himself that he wouldn't be stuck in the mud with the new tractor or caught short without gasoline during wartime rationing.

First with horses, and later with the tractor, the fields to be planted in corn were prepared by plowing the sod from last year's hayfield into dark brown curls that provided robins with an abundant spring feast of worms. Then the furrows were broken by the circular blades of a disk, and finally the clods were pulverized into small pieces by the metal fingers of a harrow. Only then were the fields ready for Daddy to run the double row corn planter that cut a groove, dropped kernels of corn from boxes on either side of its metal seat, and covered them with dirt as it moved down the row—unbelievably quaint to the modern farmer who guides a behemoth planting thirty to forty rows simultaneously.

Planting was usually finished by mid-May and twice before the middle of June the corn would be cultivated with a spring-tooth plow to kill weeds that would compete with the stalks for moisture—five trips over every foot of the fourteen or fifteen acres of corn Daddy grew each year.

After mid-June, the corn was high enough to shade the ground and prevent weeds from sprouting. By the first of July, we children could play hide and seek in the cornfields, running the length of rows that tickled our noses with the tips of their glossy leaves. Or sometimes we simply stood very still on a sunny afternoon and listened to the stalks creak and the leaves rustle in the wind. Daddy said we were hearing the corn grow, and I never quite knew if he was teasing. It was true that the stalks could grow two or three inches on a mid-summer day, but could we actually hear it happening? I never knew.

By June it was time to cut hay. The mixture of alfalfa, red and alsike clover, and timothy grass that Daddy preferred, was cut three times between early June and late August. The first cutting was the largest but contained the most timothy and clover---and weeds. This would be fed to the yearling heifers. The lush alfalfa of the second and third cutting were reserved for the milking herd.

The mower had a bar about five feet long with slots to contain individual triangular blades that Daddy sharpened every winter and between cuttings at a whetstone that he spun with a foot treadle. The mower had a seat for riding when he mowed with horses, but later it was hitched to the tractor. The cutting bar was bolted upright when he was riding to and from the field, then he had to get down and unscrew the rod to allow it to lie flat for mowing. Sometimes if the hay was thick and heavy or wet from recent rain the mower would clog and he would have to get down and clean it out with a stick. He always warned us "Never touch a mower blade with your hands."

I liked to watch him lay a swath of mown hay across the field and admire the red-winged blackbirds, their red shoulders trimmed with a brush of yellow that flashed as they dove for the insects he stirred up. Many times they built their nests in clumps of dock weeds along the fence rows, low enough that I could peek in and see the speckled eggs.

But it was the next stage of hay making that I loved. A day or two later the mown hay was turned with a side-delivery rake into neat sausage-like rolls. Nothing smells better than slightly wilted alfalfa hay. I've often wondered why someone hasn't thought to turn it into an exotic perfume.

By the time I was eleven or twelve raking hay became my job—driving our little Farmall A in its lowest gear, about the speed of a man's walk, round and around the field, creating an endless curl for the hay loader. Hot sun toasting my bare arms and legs, the marvelous aroma flooding my nostrils. I felt very grownup to be entrusted with such an important job, one of those female "Tractorettes" that the radio was praising for helping the war effort.

Hay needed two, or maybe three, days drying in the sun before it could safely be stored in the mow and every farmer had to be a weather observer for when it rained on hay in the field it leached its nutrients. Everyone knew, "Red sky in the morning, sailors take warning. Red sky at night, sailors delight." But the appearance of clouds that looked like the backs of a flock of sheep meant rain within twenty-four hours and we if we had hay ready to come in everyone would work late into the evening to beat the coming storm.

The hay-loader that hitched to the back of a wagon was a triangular machine that looked like a mammoth grasshopper from across the field. Clawed fingers picked up the windrow of hay and carried it up the slanting body of the machine until it fell over the top and dropped down onto the wagon. Willis usually forked the hay onto place on the wagon, building square corners that would prevent the load sliding off on the gentle slopes of our fields. Sometimes Daddy would hire a couple of high school boys who were trying to get their muscles in shape for the fall football season, and they would walk the field with pitchforks, collecting clumps missed by the loader or dropped off the wagon. When it came time to stow it in the mow, they were the ones who worked under the heat of the slate roof tucking the hay under the eaves with pitchforks.

Haymaking was hot sticky work and the best way to cool down was to head for the watering trough on the barn floor and plunge your arms in well above the elbows. Daddy showed me the little blue veins inside my wrists and elbows. "Blue blood is on its way back to your heart and if you chill it, within a couple of minutes your heart will be pumping it back around and cool your whole body." It sounded like magic, but it worked very well long before air conditioning.

Early one day in the summer after I graduated from the eighth grade, something broke on the mower and Daddy had to run into Granville to get some bolts at the hardware store. I can't recall why I went with him, but I remember vividly that as we started down the lane he stopped and asked, "Do you want to drive?"

Did I? I couldn't believe it. Our 1947 Plymouth was fairly new—such a pride and joy after driving our old 1934 model throughout the war. I think I jumped out and ran around to the driver's side without even taking time to answer.

Daddy showed me how you put your left foot on the brake and your right on the clutch pedal to move the gears—just like the tractor—and moved to the passenger side. I've long forgotten whether the car jumped a little the first time I engaged the gears, but I remember that I drove those four miles very slowly and carefully. After the tractor, twenty-five miles an hour seemed like sailing and I had to sit up straight and look all around to get a feel for the new situation.

There were two or three more such trips with Daddy or Mother in the next few days and then I graduated to running errands in town on my own. There was little traffic on our back roads and this was long before driver education classes. How proud I was to be entrusted with such a responsibility, but I felt none of the joyous anticipation today's teens associate with receiving their driver's license. Our car was a tool to be used for specific purposes such as going to church or running errands in town, never a plaything for the entertainment of a teenager.

By the time the first cutting of hay was in the barn the wheat field had turned to gold, ripe and ready for cutting. This was done with a binder—pulled originally by horses and later by the tractor—that cut a swath of grain and captured it on a moving canvas belt that collected a sheaf which was wrapped and tied from a ball of twine. At least that's how it was supposed to work. Maybe the technology lacked perfection, or perhaps our machine was old and balky, but I spent many an hour riding on the edge of the binder ready to tie a sheaf that the binder missed.

Sheaves dropped from the binder to the ground and Willis stacked them into shocks across the field to dry. As soon as Dave and I were old enough to carry one in each hand we helped Willis collect them so he could stand six or eight sheaves with their heads together and then fan one out on both ends to cap the shock and divert rain. The shocks might stand in the field drying for two or three weeks before the arrival of the threshing crew.

The threshing machine was an expensive piece of equipment that traveled from farm to farm with a crew of several men. It ran from a big belt laced over the revolving wheel on a huge metal tractor with cleated wheels higher than Daddy's head. What a racket it made. The men couldn't talk as they worked but had to wave their hands at each other to show what they needed.

Daddy, Willis, Uncle Doc and a couple of neighbors drove wagons to collect the sheaves from the field, pitching them up until they had a load. Then they lined up their wagons to feed the machine a steady flow, the man on the wagon pitching sheaves onto the conveyor belt with heads all facing the same direction. Sometimes I helped keep a pile of burlap bags handy for the member of the crew who was filling them with grain disgorged from a blower on the other side of the machine. From a pipe at the top of the thrasher, straw was blown unto a stack that grew higher and higher as the day wore on, and the chaff quickly found its way to stick on your sweaty face and neck.

Mother would send me out with a cool jug of water and I was fascinated by the man who controlled the blower pipe that sent the straw sailing unto a stack on the ground. He could place his forefinger through the ring on the neck of a gallon jug, swing it onto his shoulder and gulp a drink without ever losing control of the stream of straw shooting from the blower pipe in his other hand.

In the house Mother, Grandma and Aunt Gertrude would be cooking dinner—most likely ham, roasted chicken, mashed potatoes, sweet corn, green beans, plates of sliced tomatoes, loaves of bread, homemade pickles and jam, all topped off with apple, peach or cherry pie. Under the big maple tree in the back yard, boards were placed across sawhorses and covered with a bed sheet to make a table. The men splashed cold water from a bucket into the basin by the back porch to wash their hands with Lava soap before finding a place at the table. I scooted around helping to refill the pitchers of milk, water and lemonade as Mother and Grandma replenished the serving platters with seconds.

By late afternoon the last of the full grain sacks would be loaded on wagons and as the lumbering machine moved on to the next farm we were left with a golden mound of fresh straw. Threshing was over for another year and we were exhausted—by the excitement as well as the work.

But there was little rest for the weary. There was always more hay to be made and soon it was time to fill the silos. When the corn had formed ears but before the stalks and ears had turned dry, green corn was cut and piled on wagons to haul to the silo. There Daddy or Willis fed them into a machine that chopped them into pieces an inch or two long and blew them up a pipe that fed into a window at the top of the silo.

Inside the silo sections of pipe three or four feet long were snapped together to form a flexible tube that could be directed around the edge of the circular silo like pouring batter into a cake pan. At first it was Mother's job to direct this blower, but by the time we were eight or ten

Dave and I took over, stomping the silage down with our bare feet, and unhooking sections of blower as the silo became fuller and higher. I've heard since that gases can build up inside a silo and overcome persons working there, but I'm sure my parents never knew of such hazards and in all probability there were enough cracks between the boards of our wooden silos to prevent such danger.

We went back to school before corn harvest began in earnest, but the process was similar to cutting wheat. Corn stalks were cut and bound together and stacked in shocks across the field. It produced a picturesque sight that can still be seen in some Amish communities. There was an old man whose name I no longer remember who walked out from town every fall to husk corn. He moved from shock to shock, kneeling or sitting beside it to strip the ear from each stalk with a special glove with a metal hook in the palm like some evil creature, piling the ears on the ground in a golden mound and re-shocking the stalks.

Willis would haul the corn to the crib while Daddy sowed next year's wheat with a seeder that he wore over his shoulder like a set of bagpipes, squeezing the canvas bag of seed with his elbow as he cranked the handle to spin the blades that cast seeds several feet on either side as he walked briskly across the field.

Mother's garden had its own seasons. In addition to keeping the books for Sharon View Dairy and cooking for the family—together with the milk tester, the threshing crew, and a few boys helping with the haying—her summer schedule included planting and weeding the garden, as well as picking and preserving its produce.

This began in early May with rhubarb that was canned for pies, and continued into June with strawberries and raspberries that were turned into thick, sweet jam. Even as toddlers Dave and I were enticed into helping pick by the fact that we could eat as many juicy berries as we liked and still have plenty for jam. Our strawberry patch was in the garden, but there were always plenty of raspberries and blackberries growing wild, particularly in the hollow up on the hill around the spring. Here the brambles formed a thicket crisscrossed by groundhog burrows that allowed their occupants a feast without fear of being exposed to predators. But there were plenty for all and we always returned with full pails and purple lips and fingers.

When sugar was rationed during the war, it became a challenge to find a way to preserve the jam that we always spread liberally on bread and toast. During the war, Mother patriotically tried the recommended substitutes. I remember the results as more like soup than jam, so we saved our sugar ration stamps to make jam and used honey, Karo corn syrup, or molasses for everything else. I hated the Karo syrup poured on cornflakes for breakfast, which created gooey globs we kids resisted mightily.

But it was the vegetables and fruits for pies that kept the big canning kettle boiling all summer long—peas, cherries, green beans, lima beans, beets, sweet corn, peaches, tomatoes. Sometimes we helped Mother shell peas or lima beans, usually in the shade of the back porch where screens kept out the flies. Peas were the most fun because you could pop the pod open and run your finger along the line of peas to make them soar—with luck into the pan rather than on the floor.

The Mason glass quart canning jars had aluminum lids that were sealed with a red rubber ring. Mother would boil the empty jars and lids to sterilize them, then lift them out of the boiling water with long-handled tongs, fill them with the prepared vegetables or fruit, cover them with boiling water or syrup, seal them loosely and replace them in the boiling water to simmer for a precise time depending on the contents. Finally she would lift them carefully to a wooden rack in the corner of the kitchen counter to cool slowly.

Needless to say, the constantly steaming kettle added greatly to the heat and humidity of the kitchen. Fruits like peaches were simply peeled, placed in the jars and covered with boiling syrup, but vegetables were partially cooked before canning. Beets were the most fun because you simply cut off the tops leaving an inch or so of stems, placed them a big kettle and boiled them until they were fork tender. Then you cooled them with enough cold water so that you could handle them, cut off the tops and root, and slide the outer skin off with your fingers like peeling skin from a sunburn.

It must have taken hundreds of these cans to supply our family with fruits and vegetables all winter long for I seem to remember eighty or a hundred cans of tomatoes alone. I can still see the gleaming jars on wooden shelves along the cellar wall, five or six shelves high and each two rows of cans deep. I never saw Mother pause to admire her handiwork. Perhaps it was simply hard work that she was glad to have done. I do remember that our garden began to shrink after the war when tins cans of fruits and vegetables became available at the grocery, and before I graduated from high school my folks had purchased a chest freezer to replace the meat locker in town and mother began to freeze peaches and peas and lima beans.

Of course it is impossible to remember the tasks of my childhood without comparing the conveniences of modern life. I'm certain that the mornings and evenings my father and Willis milked, before and after long hours in the field, equal any dot.com entrepreneur managing his own business and making frequent flights across the country.

My mother's hours gardening, preserving food, and handling the Sharon View Dairy accounts exceeded most employed wives and mothers of today, but stopping at the delicatessen for dinner was never an option. We didn't have such convience stores in either Newark or Granville. Yet I always felt my parents were in control of their lives. No one spoke of burnout—perhaps because they were both boss and worker.

Throughout our childhood we learned the skills we would need as adults from watching and helping our parents. The fall I started the eighth grade, mother told me that I would be in charge of getting dinner for the family after I came home from school. For years I had been helping her by making a jello salad, a pot of soup, or peeling and mashing the potatoes, but how proud I was to be counted on to make the whole dinner. Like my mother and grandmother before me, I never questioned that it was the woman's role to cook meals for the family. I had never eaten in a restaurant or seen a male chef.

11

◆━━━◆◆◆◆◆◆◆◆◆◆◆◆◆◆◆◆◆◆◆◆◆◆◆◆◆◆◆◆◆◆◆◆◆━━━◆

Robin Hood's Merry Band

I watch the back of my grandson's head, bopping and swaying to a melody only he can hear through the headset attached to either ear. His eyes on the computer monitor and his fingers on its mouse, he controls screen images faster than I can follow. I wonder. When did recorded music become background noise, simply to fill the gaps while you are busy doing something else?

I smile—imagining to myself how Stefan would be convulsed with laughter if by some miracle he were transported back sixty years to our kitchen where mother is drying dishes and Dave and I, with elbows resting on the kitchen table to cup our chins in our hands, are deeply engrossed in listening to the trials of *The Great Gildersleeve.* Of course, Gildersleeve was funny and we'd be laughing ourselves, but my grandson would find it hilarious that we would gather around simply to listen to the radio on the shelf.

We didn't even have one of those big Philco consoles to sit in the living room, just a brown plastic bundle about the size of a shoe box with rounded corners and knobs for turning it on or off and selecting a

105

station. Actually we didn't really need the second knob. The only station that came in clearly was WLW from Cincinnati. Our link to the world of entertainment sat at the shelf over our kitchen table where Mother could hear Lowell Thomas say "Good evening ladies and gentlemen," and deliver the news of the world. Daddy had a similar radio in the barn—on a shelf over the feed cart—to catch the news and weather report or soothe the cows with country blue grass melodies. Those were the days when the headliners of the *Saturday Night Jamboree* from Renfro Valley, Kentucky were superstars.

But my favorite was *A Date with Judy*, and if I had homework on Tuesday night I'd hurry to finish so I would be allowed to listen. This ditsy teenager was everything I wanted to be---popular with boys, so many invitations to go somewhere and do something that she could hardly choose.

My radio era would be impossible to explain to todays' pre-teens, but the more I think about it the more I realize it's only the technology that has changed. What did we do for fun when we couldn't flop down on the couch to watch TV or log on Facebook to see what our buddies are up to?

We glued ourselves to the radio for Cleveland Indians baseball games, cheered when Bob Feller struck out a batter, and could hardly contain our pride when the Indians beat the Red Sox to win the American League pennant. The difference is seeing as well as hearing, but that's big.

If we weren't gathered round the radio, we might pick up the party-line telephone. It wasn't intended to be entertainment but it was often our best source of local news. Crank phones and real live operators to ring your number were gone before my time. During my childhood we had a phone on the wall—black, of course—with a rotary-dial and a bell-shaped earpiece that you lifted from its hook. A similarly shaped but smaller mouthpiece on the wall forced you to lean forward to talk.

There were ten families on our party line, which was pretty standard in rural communities. When the phone rang for one of our neighbors, our phone buzzed and you could tell from the number of buzzes who was getting a call. Nobody wanted to hear old Mrs. Norpell tell her daughter about how bad her rheumatism was hurting, but if a call sounded like it might be interesting you could quietly lift the receiver and listen. The trick was to hold down the hook with your right hand, lift off the receiver with your left and then gently, gently release the hook.

Even then, if it was the oldest Claggett girl talking to her boyfriend you might hear her say, "Can I pluueesse have a little privacy here?"

Sometimes I just waited quietly, hoping they would forget me and go on talking.

"I know you're there. I can hear you breathing."

Oh well, I could always replace the receiver and try again in a few minutes.

Sometimes mother would pick up the phone and find a couple of neighbors talking and join in just to catch up on the news. If she needed to use the phone for an emergency and someone was just talking and talking, she might pick up the receiver every couple of minutes, getting a bit noisier each time hoping that they will catch the hint that someone else wanted to use the phone. But in a real emergency, she could break in and say "I need to phone the vet," and know that the neighbors would immediately hang up—but perhaps pick up again after they heard the ring to check that she actually did.

Party phone lines were a test of human nature at its best and at its most aggravating.

Farm children were expected to entertain ourselves. Adults rarely had time to join or supervise play, and until we were about ten or eleven we weren't allowed to roam the half mile or so to visit neighboring children.

Summer offered endless possibilities, but for Dave and me the creek usually won. Actually we had two creeks—our first adventures were in the small drainage ditch between the fields east of the house that was within view of mother's kitchen windows. A large culvert carried its shallow water beneath the road and this was the perfect place to find crawdads— little crayfish about three or four inches long with pincher claws, flat tails, and four pairs of legs on their body.

Wading in barefoot we would use a small stick to root them from their comfortable hiding places among the pebbles, laughing with delight at the speed with which they could propel themselves backwards. Or we could nudge our stick between one's pinchers until he felt threatened enough to grab it. Then you could slowly lift him high out of the water—until he fell off, hitting the surface with a splash and disappearing into the sandy bottom with a muddy flurry. We never intended to be cruel and certainly never considered the crayfish's point of view. They were simply toys that God had created for our amusement.

In the winter, one of the advantages of a home on the hillside was great sledding. One of the best Christmas presents ever was the year Dave and I jointly received a real sled. No more borrowed washtub or loose boards from the barn. This was a bona fide "Red Rider" painted a shiny red with metal runners, a wooden seat big enough for both of us to ride at the same time, and a steering board where the person in front placed their feet and pushed right or left to turn. If we wore the lane down to gravel, we simply headed for one of the hills in the pasture and started a new track.

I didn't know then that the classic image of a tomboy is a girl hanging from a tree limb by her knees, but I learned early to appreciate the secret world of leafy branches.

Climbing trees was nearly as easy as learning to walk because the cherry tree outside our dining room window began branching three or four feet from the ground. It was like climbing stair steps to leafy balconies among the branches where you could rest your back against the trunk in a two-o'clock position, help yourself to your fill when cherries were ripe, and daydream or read until you heard your name being called.

The maple tree that shaded the living room had higher branches and it took a boost from Dave to get me up and then a hand from me to pull him up. But once we were there we had a wonderful view of the couch and chairs in the living room when the ladies of mother's church circle were having tea and cookies. And what fun it was to sit ever so still and watch them departing down the walk beneath us in their hats and gloves, expressing their thanks to my mother and their regrets at not having seen "your lovely children."

When we were a little older and rambled as far as the next door neighbor's big woods that adjoined our pasture, we discovered the glory of wild grapevines. Towering oaks supported vines as thick as Daddy's wrist that we could grab, pull back as far as we could and then run to swing freely.

The edge of those woods was the site of the wildest plan of my childhood. It all began when Dave got a BB gun for his birthday. My father was never a hunter, although he would occasionally allow an old man who walked out from town with his shotgun to hunt groundhogs. Dave and I had little knowledge of guns. Perhaps one of his buddies at school had a BB gun, for he begged for one and must have been about ten by the time my parents considered him old enough to use it properly.

At first we—for he would let me have a turn if I signed my life away and agreed to do some of his chores—practiced aiming at a tin can that Daddy nailed to one of the fence posts behind the garden. I'm not sure how we got the idea to shoot some of the pigeons that rested on the ridge of the barn. I suspect Dave was showing off for our friend Stewart, but the idea for a campfire was mine. I read something about the king and queen serving squab, a fancy name for roasted pigeons, to their guests when they had a hunting party at their castle in Scotland before the war. My plan was to pluck the feathers just like a chicken and put the pigeon on a stick to roast like the marshmellows at Girl Scout camp. From the ground, those fluffy pigeons looked so fat and delicious. But we had a serious problem. The BB gun never killed a pigeon, just made them scatter and fly away. No campfire, no squab.

Perhaps if our neighborhood had included girls my age I would have become a lady rather than a tomboy. Goodness knows I endured hours with mother rolling my straight blond hair on her curling iron and then teasing curls around her finger until she had created an approximation of Shirley Temple curls. That dimpled movie darling made my life and thousands of others miserable in the late 1930s and early 40s. But my curls refused to bounce and by the time Sunday School was over they would be drooping badly.

As luck would have it, the only girl within a two-mile radius of our house was Sally Beck and she was three years older—and four grades ahead of me having skipped a grade. We sometimes played together in the summer but that was quite an age barrier.

Her brother Stewart was my age, and together with Paul and Larry Claggett—cousins who lived a mile in either direction from our house and were in Dave's class—we formed a gang by the time Stewart and I reached the fourth grade.

The Becks moved to the country when we were in the first grade, not to a farm but to a house about a half mile from ours. Mr. Beck had a laboratory in town where he made false teeth for dentists. I'll never forget the first time I visited their house and saw that Stewart kept a set of false teeth on a shelf in his room. That was really impressive and Dave and I never questioned that he was our leader.

About fourth or fifth grade Stewart and my class read a child's version of Robin, and became obsessed with this chivalrous bandit who robbed the rich and gave to the poor. It suited our sense of adventure and justice. The creek that ran between our house and theirs was thickly lined with elderberry bushes that created a perfect Sherwood Forest. Stewart was Robin Hood and I, of course, played Maid Marian. Dave, Paul and Larry took turns being Friar Tuck and the hapless victims that we captured and tied their arms and legs.

We had far fewer holidays from school, and none of the parent-teacher conference days students now take for granted.

Halloween wasn't a big deal until we were about ten or twelve and then our gang was allowed to go trick or treating along Sharon Valley Road. This was far from the candy collection orgies of today. We prepared by shelling several ears of corn and carrying a paper bag full so we could dip in for a handful and announce our arrival by throwing it against our neighbors' windows while screaming "Trick or Treat!" Grains of corn produce a startling noise, but I suspect our victims were forewarned by footsteps and giggles on their porch.

Houses in the country were some distance apart. We usually only visited three or four houses where we would be invited in for cider and doughnuts, or hot chocolate and candy corn. It would never have occurred to our parents that we might be poisoned. Only once do I recall performing a trick that could be considered mildly destructive, and it involved a carefully placed pile of dog poop in the mailbox of an older neighbor who never invited us in.

Valentine's Day was the only holiday I recall celebrating in school. Our teacher would cover a cardboard box with red crepe paper, stick on a few valentines for decoration, and cut a slit in the top for each of us to deposit our valentines. Valentines cost a penny each at the Five and Dime and gushed with sentiments such as a spotted puppy with a red heart tied around his neck saying "Be my pet." You were supposed to have one for everyone in your class, but you never signed your name. We girls spent a lot of time guessing who sent which one, especially if it said LOVE. And someone usually spilled their Koolaid on the red crepe paper ribbons decorating the table making them bleed.

Strange as it may seem to modern youth, we spent little time around home playing traditional ball games. Yes, I can remember a baseball diamond that we occasionally created with dried patches of cow dung serving as bases in the stubble of the harvested hayfield. But we didn't have enough players for a team and our games were just glorified batting practice.

We had a croquet set with posts and wickets that we could set up in the yard, but our yard had many bumps and gullies underneath the grass and we delighted in seeing an opponent's ball roll into a ditch, knowing that we could easily send our own there, hit it and earn the right to knock it as far away as possible.

Despite such cut throat competition, croquet was one of the few approved activities for Sunday afternoon. Reading was fine, but movies were not allowed — a fact that caused me much consternation when I reached high school and had friends who could drive. Sunday was a day of rest or visiting with family. Even if there was hay mowed and Monday was threatening rain, Sunday in our family was a day you did not do anything except the necessary morning and evening milking chores. If it was a hot summer day and Dave and I were playing croquet, Mother and Daddy and Grandma were likely sitting in the glider with oilcloth covered cushions, their feet moving it slowly back and forth to create a bit of breeze.

Sometimes one or more of the adults would sit there after supper, enjoying the cool of the evening while Dave and I gleefully chased fireflies and placed them in a glass jar. We always thought we could catch enough to create a flashlight, but the poor creatures piled up upon themselves in their captivity and died before morning. Later, when I studied Hindu theology in college, I thought about my Christian upbringing and wondered why no one had raised questions about reverence for all living creatures. Perhaps life and death were too common on a farm—tomcats killed baby kittens and Mother killed chickens for Sunday dinner. We never discussed the morality of human supremacy.

As I watch the organized sports activities of my grandchildren, I wonder that we did not suffer from boredom. But my memories are the opposite. It seems to me that our days were filled with discoveries. We developed a sense of independence and responsibility designing our own entertainments, waging our battles, and working out compromises.

12

---•••◆••• ••◆•• •••◆---

Jesus Loves Me

The compromise that led my Methodist father and Presbyterian mother to join the Granville Baptist Church still strikes me as odd, but it happened before I was born and surrounded my childhood as a given. From the distance of adulthood I suspect it had more to do with sociability than theology.

As a member of the Northern Baptist Convention, the congregation in which I grew up was more liberal than modern stereotypes of Baptist theology. Denison University had been founded by these Baptists a century before and during the 1930s and 1940s the affiliation was still quite strong. The liberal arts college gave our congregation a strong missionary heritage and the tradition of employing highly educated ministers.

Our church was a large limestone building with an auditorium that could seat as many as 2000 persons for services. I can't say for certain that church attendance was still compulsory for Denison students, but when school was in session it was frequently filled to capacity. If we arrived just as the service was starting—or a minute or two later, as we often did—our regular pew three rows from the back of the center section might already be filled. This wasn't really an assigned place, but over the years the two to three hundred church members habitually sat in the same place and regular members knew and respected that as students might not.

The fan-shaped auditorium was divided into three sections by side aisles, all of which sloped toward the front platform that held the pulpit and two throne-like chairs covered in red velvet for the minister and the deacon who read the scripture. In the center, an oval arch with red velvet draperies concealed an alcove containing the baptistery, and above all was the choir loft which usually held about thirty robed choristers.

It was a setting of late Victorian formality with varnished oak woodwork, classical supporting columns, and variegated plaster painted in shades of turquoise and peach. The oak pews had a high gloss varnish that was perfect for sliding over and making room for one more person. Daddy wore his black suit, and like all of the women Mother wore a hat and gloves. Dave and I were always shined and polished, which in my case involved a much dreaded session with the curling iron to turn my straight flyaway hair into a poor imitation of the Shirley Temple curls that were the fashion for little girls.

There was no day care for small children during services. From my earliest memory we attended church with my parents, but thanks to the noon meal for Denison students the service was confined to an hour and could be relied upon to end promptly. We loved to join in the hymns during the early part of the service, but when the minister settled into his sermon we could count on mother to open her purse and give Dave and me each a pencil and piece of paper that we placed on the hymn book to quietly sit and draw. I think our parents expected us to soak up the spiritual atmosphere by osmosis. If I leaned forward to catch the eye of my friend Louise, whose family sat in the same row on the right hand side, I would soon get a stern look from Mother to sit back.

All the ladies that Mother stopped to talk with after church seemed terribly old to me—at least the age I am now. She had a special sensitivity for shut-ins and when we were quite small it was a treat every spring to make May baskets to deliver to a half dozen of these ladies on the first day of May. This involved a trip to our woods where we would collect moss to line glass jars that became small terrariums. Mother liked these because they lasted longer than open baskets. Mother knew where to look for blood root and we had to dig it gently to avoid cutting and making its roots bleed. We centered each jar with one of its delicate white blossoms and surrounded it with moss and sprigs of ground cherry with a few bright red berries.

I understood the spirit of giving that Mother was attempting to instill, but only much later did I realize that her May baskets were also a way of emphasizing our role as a farm family in an academic community. Having access to a woods with wildflowers made us unique.

After the end of gas rationing, Mother would often take us in and drop us off to attend Sunday School, which had classes before church. Then she would return to help Daddy finish the chores and ride back with him for church services.

I liked having the teacher read us stories from the Bible and let us cut out and make pictures to illustrate these stories, but I especially liked vacation Bible school in the summer when for a week we would go every morning to hear stories, play games, and learn verses and hymns for a children's program in front of the entire congregation at the end of the week. My favorite song was *Jesus Loves Me,* and we all sang "Jesus loves me, this I know" with an innocence and absolute certainty that I now find amazing.

Perhaps a half dozen times a year our church celebrated communion, with the deacons solemnly passing first silver plates of bread cubes from pew to pew, followed by trays of grape juice served in little glass goblets about the size of Daddy's thumb. When we were little I watched Mother and Daddy carefully remove a glass and hold it until everyone had been served and the minister invited them to share the blood of Christ together. Then there would be clinking all over the church as people placed their empty glasses in the little holder with three holes on the back of the pew in front of us. We were supposed to bow our heads and close our eyes and think about God forgiving our sins, but I always peeked between my fingers to watch Daddy's Adam's Apple bobble as he swallowed the bread without chewing it.

No one was supposed to take communion until they were old enough to accept Christ as their Savior. Our church did not believe in infant baptism, but accepted converts who had reached the age of reason and professed their faith. In the seventh grade, our Sunday School teacher spent several weeks preparing us and then we each had an interview with the minister to see if we understood how Jesus had died to save us. It was a very solemn time and we looked forward with a little fear to the day when we would be immersed in the baptismal in front of the congregation.

I'd seen some of my older friends baptized. The red draperies concealing the baptismal were pulled back from both sides to frame the minister and the supplicant standing up to their knees in a tank of water about the size of a bathtub. But I had never learned how to swim and I was secretly afraid of having my head under water. What if I started to splutter when he dunked me? Rev. Maxwell promised each of us that he would hold our nose just as we went under.

The boys wore white shirts and dark pants and we girls white gowns, loose like a nightgown. No jewelry. No shoes. Just our bodies having the sins of the world washed away.

When my turn came, I waded in and crossed my hands over my chest the way our Sunday School teacher had shown us.

When the curtains opened, Rev. Maxwell looked into my eyes and asked, "Virginia Mary Evans, do you accept Jesus Christ as your Lord and Savior?"

I whispered, "I do"

"I baptize you in the name of the Father, the Son, and The Holy Ghost." With a swish I was under the water and lifted back up so quickly I barely knew what happened.

The curtain was already down by the time I brushed my wet hair out of my eyes and reached for my teacher's hand to climb out dripping and shivering.

Why had I thought that I would feel magically different? Wasn't I supposed to? I didn't have time to think about it as I hurried with my classmates to dry my hair and change clothes for the punch and cookies reception with our parents after the service ended.

So now I was allowed to take communion.

Even more important, when I reached seventh grade I was eligible to join BYF, the Baptist Youth Fellowship that met every Sunday night.

I was the only one out of a dozen or fifteen members who didn't attend school in Granville and I suppose that made me a bit exotic, but I just felt shy. Most of their fathers were professors at Denison, but a couple lived in the Baptist home for sons and daughters of missionaries. One of the boys had grown up in Africa and had never seen snow until that winter.

Most of our time in BYF we learned about other religions, did service projects or had social activities. First we would study another religion like Catholicism or Judaism for three or four weeks and then we would make a trip to attend services.

There was a Catholic Church in Newark but we had to go to

Columbus to attend a Jewish synagogue. It was fascinating in both places to see all the lighted candles and hear the singsong chanting in a foreign language, but I didn't quite understand why Catholics talked to God in Latin and Jews in Hebrew. Afterwards we asked Mr. Dewey—a Denison staff member who was our leader—a lot of questions. For the first time, I learned about what Hitler had done to Jews during the war and we tried to understand how people who called themselves Christians could hate someone just because they had a different religion.

I found it fascinating that there were so many ways to worship God. Mother and Daddy let me go on these trips but they didn't like for me to talk about what I'd seen. I thought about that some years later when I first saw *South Pacific* and heard Rogers and Hammerstein's lyrics:

> *You've got to be taught to hate and fear,*
> *you've got to be taught from year to year.*
> *You've got to be taught to be afraid*
> *of people who's eyes are oddly made*
> *and people who's skin is a different shade.*
> *You've got to be taught before it's too late*
> *before you are six or seven or eight.*
> *You've got to be carefully taught.*

My childhood exposure to Catholics and Jews was superficial and it would be a college course that first introduced me to Buddhists and Muslims, and Hindus, but I was still lucky to be having childhood experiences my parents had missed.

Only later did I wonder about the contradictions of enthusiastically singing *Jesus Loves Me* one moment and shouting "Don't leave room for Tojo" as we piled into the car after Vacation Bible School.

World War II was a pervasive presence during my childhood. Things like gas rationing were a fact of life, and we were thoroughly brainwashed to make no extra trips and travel with a full car. Hitchhiking was an accepted form of transportation and it was unpatriotic to pass someone—particularly a young man in uniform—with an arm raised and thumb extended without stopping to offer a ride.

An empty seat was a space for Uncle Tojo, that vicious dark-haired Jap who represented the enemy. Of course, America was also fighting Hitler and caricatures that emphasized his bristly mustache were common, but the most extensive propaganda was against those treacherous slanty-eyed Japs who had bombed our troops at Pearl Harbor.

I can well remember the newspaper cartoons and the war bond posters. But I can't remember our Sunday School teachers ever mentioning the propaganda about our wartime enemies. How odd, when I recall Nancy Toy, a Japanese-American who was a member of our BYF. Her father taught at Denison and she was very bright and very quiet. What an opportunity we missed to have discussed and shared the pain her family must have experienced during the war years.

Yes, I feel some pangs of guilt that the social activities associated with BYF are more intense memories than the discussions of religion, or the Saturday mornings doing spring cleanup in the yards of elderly church members.

In the fall BYF held a hayride—a hay covered wagon pulled by a tractor to a barn north of town where we had cider and played games. I suppose this was more of a treat for all of the town kids than this farm girl, but I remember it vividly because on the way back Dougal Pendergast held my hand! That had never happened before and I wasn't sure how to act. But everyone was talking and laughing and noticing who was holding hands with who. It just seemed right for the night. Dougal was tall with curly blond hair, thick glasses, and he played the horn. If this seems like a story without an ending, it was. We seventh-graders were too young to think about dating and I think Dougal stopped coming to BYF soon after that.

Louise Titus was my best friend in BYF and it was at her house that I attended my first slumber party. A half dozen girls, rolling our hair in curlers—how did we ever manage to sleep on those fashionable instruments of torture? We talked much of the night on weighty topics such as who had fallen off the roof— our term for menstruation—with the half who had begun their monthly periods sharing much information to the questions of those who had not yet become real women.

It was also with Louise that I shared the adventure of a trip to Green Lake, Wisconsin to attend the national BYF camp. It must have been an honor to be chosen for I marvel that my parents, who had never taken us on a trip even across Ohio, allowed two thirteen-year-old girls to make this trip alone by train.

There were no passenger trains through Newark or Granville and Louise's parents took us to northern Ohio to meet the Pullman to Chicago. The train traveled through the night and how strange it was to walk down an aisle with nothing but curtains on either side, most of them pulled because people were already sleeping. The conductor tossed our suitcases on the upper and lower berths that were to be ours, but we ended up giggling together in the lower bunk, too excited to sleep a wink.

Just about daylight we arrived in the huge Chicago station where we had to change for a train to Green Lake. I'm not sure who helped us, but we must have had a group leader who made the connection and we arrived safely and had a marvelous time at camp.

When my parents arrived at the end of the week to pick us up, they were horrified to find I was with a group in a rowboat out on the lake, knowing that I had never learned to swim. Actually, the Green Lake water was too cold for swimming and I had not worried about drowning or thought it necessary to confess my inadequacy to the counselors.

13

Camp Wakatomika and the Hartford Fair

I was born again the day I became a Brownie! Light brown uniform that buttoned down the front, beanie cap, and shiny gold cloverleaf pin with an elfin Brownie. I belonged!

If my parents sacrificed to acquire these symbols, I never realized it. I just felt I had been given a special status in the group that met after school a couple of times each month. Try as I might, I can't recall what we actually did, although I have vague images of projects such as tinting macaroni with food coloring and gluing it to an empty glass peanut butter jar. A gift for Mother's Day perhaps?

I do remember vividly the day we flew up to become Girl Scouts. Girls who were already Scouts formed a circle as they sang and danced around the Brownies clustered in the center. We had each been instructed to wear an item of clothing that we could remove like butterflies emerging from their cocoons to join the singing circle.

Most of the girls had a scarf or sweater that was quickly shed as they moved into the circle, but Mother had decided that I should wear a jumper over my new green Scout uniform. This probably was a more realistic interpretation of the cocoon/butterfly metamorphoses, but all I remember is standing in the center of the singing circle tugging and struggling to get the tight jumper over my head. Those moments lasted forever. I was not only the last to fly up, but mortified as only a pre-teen can be about how difficult and different my life was compared to others.

The very best thing about becoming a Girl Scout was that you were eligible to attend camp for a week in the summer. Camp Wakatomika was fifteen or twenty miles from our home in a wooded area with a large stream, and contained several canvas tents clustered around a central wooden dining hall. Our tent had a wood floor and a half dozen canvas cots that we assembled with wood sticks at head and toe to hold the canvas tight. A rope ran between the two poles that supported the tent and gave us a place to hang a few clothes. Our counselor, Pat "White Feather"— all the counselors had Indian names—slept on a cot in the center, in front of the flaps that we tied open during the day and closed at night. It helped to know she was there in case a bear or something crashed out of the woods during the middle of the night.

Wakatomika Creek had a deep place that we used as a swimming hole. Like most of the girls however, I had never been around water enough to learn how to swim. We splashed and paddled and had a tremendously good time. After lunch was nap time when everyone was supposed to be on their bunk with their feet off the floor, even though no one ever slept. It seemed like such a silly rule, and we tested it in every way possible.

"Sally, get back on your own bed."

"But you said, 'In your bunks and feet off the floor.' I'm resting with Mary Lou."

"In your <u>own</u> cot. Now!"

Sally slowly obeyed as the whispers and giggles faded. But soon there was stomping, someone walking on the floor. Jan had dropped one leg over the edge of her cot on the tent side and was stomping the floor.

"Jan, no walking."

"But I'm on my bunk."

"Both feet up."

We could all hear her deep sigh as she stretched both legs full length on her bunk. For a moment all was quiet and then there came the distinct sound of scratching against the tent.

"Listen! Something's trying to get in."

"I'll bet it's a raccoon."

"No, probably just a squirrel."

"Go chase it away, Pat."

With a groan our tormented counselor rose and ducked through the flap. I quickly showed the others the stick I had been using to scratch the canvas beside my bunk, eliciting an admiring chorus of yelps and giggles. But Pat was back. "Jennie let me have that stick," and she threw it into the woods.

"All right, QUIET TIME, everybody."

In the afternoon the dining hall became a craft classroom. The very first thing we all wanted to make was a lanyard. All of the counselors wore plastic lanyards around their necks, woven so they could slide the tin whistle hooked on the end up or down, blowing it to attract the attention of an errant swimmer, or to indicate a player out at first base. Lanyards were symbols of authority and we all had to have one. You picked two colors like red and white, or blue and yellow, and began by looping them at the hook that would eventually hold your whistle or keys. Anchoring this to a nail in the side of the dining hall, you braided and braided, testing it around your neck until your cord was long enough, and then one of the counselors would help you braid a square around your cord to form the slide.

But we didn't get our whistles until we were leaving camp headed for home. Our counselors were patient but not foolhardy.

After supper came campfire—the very best time of day. We usually had a theme and dressed up as Indians, or hobos, or pioneers. We sat on logs pulled into a circle around the spot where the counselors built a campfire within an arc of stones. Each tent usually spent part of the afternoon working on a skit to present, and Chief Twila—the camp director—always had a story about olden times around Wakatomika Creek. Our favorite was about the Indian maiden who climbed to the top of the hill every full moon, chanting for the safe return of her warrior lover. By this time it would be dark and "Singing Wind" would teach us songs as the embers of the fire died down—*Kookabarra Sits on the Old Gum Tree, I've Been Workin' on the Railroad, She'll Be Comin' Round the Mountain.*

I was nine and this was my first time away from home. All day long camp was wonderful, but when we got back to our tent and Pat's battery-powered lantern shot shadows against the side of the tent, I got the saddest feeling. By the time we got into our pajamas, settled into our blankets, and Pat turned out the light, I couldn't control the lump in my throat. Tears streamed down my cheeks as I tried to choke my sobs so the others wouldn't hear. I wanted to go home. Pat sat on my cot and stoked my hair. Eventually I went to sleep.

The next year I couldn't wait to go back. Our tent had been chosen to try out a new fiberglass tent that the local Owens-Corning company had developed for soldiers to use in the war. But the second day there was a phone call and I had to go home. Mother was in the hospital and Uncle Frank had come over to help milk the cows. I was the only one besides Daddy who knew how much feed to give each of the cows and Daddy was at the hospital in Columbus with Mother. This time I cried because I had to go home—partly because I would miss the fun at camp, and partly because Mother was in the hospital and I was afraid.

Daddy told us that Mother had a lump in her breast and that the surgeon was going to operate and remove it. It didn't sound too serious, and when Mother came home a week later her arm was sore but she didn't act particularly sick. It was a number of years before I realized the significance of a radical mastectomy and marveled at my mother's seeming nonchalance about the procedure with my brother and me. I'm sure she intended not to worry us, but I never really knew about her own feelings. As she lived into her nineties without further treatment I sometimes wondered whether her lump had indeed been a malignant tumor that had fortunately been found early or whether medical practice of the 1940s assumed the worst and offered a radical solution.

It was inevitable that I would become a 4-H Club member. This was one of the programs Mother had conducted in Licking County before she was married. After she quit, she felt she should not serve as a volunteer 4-H Club leader as that might be difficult for her replacement. A neighbor about a mile up the road was our leader, but try as I might I can't remember the name of our club. Most clubs had cute names and we were probably something like the Sharon Valley Stitchers and Bakers—for we had the choice of sewing or cooking projects. New clothes were more appealing than food so I chose to sew.

First year 4-Hers had no choice. Everyone had to hem a linen tea towel, make a hot pan holder, and a pin cushion. At first I thought this was a joke. At our house we dried dishes with old terrycloth hand towels that had been washed so many times they were thin and soft. Mother grabbed casseroles or cookie sheets from the oven with a folded washcloth and when I was sewing I stuck pins in any handy scrap of material. But mother dutifully bought supplies and I began the tedious business of ironing a hem on the linen towel and painstakingly stitching it with tiny hand stitches. It was a messy effort but I survived and the next year was promoted to making an apron—a garment neither Mother or I ever wore.

Needless to say I was elated when at age eleven I was finally allowed to make a skirt---a glorious red and white print skirt with a full gathered waist. Mother completed an outfit for me by making a white blouse with a drawstring neckline that tied with a red ribbon. Because I was growing rapidly that year, Mother advised me to double the skirt hem over twice so I could let it out once and still wear the skirt again next year. 4-H projects were graded for quality, and I approached the judging that preceded the county fair feeling like a queen. I'm sure the lady judge made some positive remark about my skirt's becoming color or something, but all I remember is her holding the double hem of my skirt and commenting, "Well, I'd like to see this when you grow into it." I was completely deflated. I knew Mother would never say that, but neither would she criticize her successor.

The next year I was finally allowed to make my first dress from a real store-bought pattern. It was my choice, but why Mother and my leader allowed me to choose plaid fabric and an incompatible pattern with a three-tiered ruffled skirt and a bodice with a scalloped neckline, I'll never know. Any one of those challenges would have been difficult for a beginner. But I truly loved that dress and worked and worked to get the plaid lined up right. I had to hurry to finish because I was going to a church camp in Wisconsin and would be gone until the week before the fair. When I finished the hem and tried it on for the last time, I could hardly believe it. This was the dress of my dreams! I told my leader I wanted to take it with me to church camp but would be back in time for the fair.

She was shocked. "You can't wear your 4-H project before judging!"

"But I want to take it to camp. I'll wash it and iron it before the fair."

"If you take that dress and wear it before judging you'll receive an incomplete on your project and it will count against our whole club."

I was shattered but stubborn. The dress went with me to camp and I left the 4-H sewing club with an incomplete on my record. But it left an indelible memory about teachable moments that served me well later in life.

I was already a member of the countywide 4-H dairy club that had more boys than girls and was more fun. When I turned ten Daddy let me choose a heifer calf for my very own with the understanding that I would raise her as a 4-H project. He would provide the feed and I would take care of her and train her to show at the fair, and any prize money I earned or any calves she had after she grew up would be mine to sell and save money for college.

That was how I got "Puddintain"—an affectionate nickname Daddy had called me when I was little. I had outgrown it, but somehow it seemed just right for my baby calf.

Puddintain was mostly white with reddish brown ears and speckles along her neck. I washed her flanks endlessly with Fels Naptha soap to remove the yellow manure stains, and taught her to lead with a rope halter that we learned to make at a 4-H meeting. Round and round the barnyard we went, me walking backwards as we were expected to do in the show ring, stopping frequently so she would become accustomed to standing with her feet squarely together as poised as any human model on the runway.

Jennie showing Puddintain at Hartford Fair

When it was our turn to host a 4-H meeting, Dave and I showed off our heifers, proud of their good behavior. But for the most part, our meetings were social events. As soon as the business was done we adjourned to the serious business of *Kick the Can*, an elaborate form of hide and seek that involved a person designated IT stationed near an empty tin can under the lightpole by the garden. Everyone else hid, but the object was to sneak back and kick the can before the person who was it could tag you and make you it. Such an intricate process required the it person to wander far enough from the pole to tempt kickers into dashing from the shadows to kick the can, but remaining close enough to tag them before they reached the target.

After much running and shouting we would adjourn for refreshments such as cookies and homemade ice cream. The latter was a special treat that only happened a few times each summer. Mother used nothing but eggs, milk, sugar and vanilla. No one questioned the safety of eating raw eggs in those days, and our homemade ice cream was always vanilla. Daddy and our 4-H leaders would place ice in the bucket that surrounded the canister of ice cream, sprinkle it with salt and take turns cranking the handle until it became too hard to move. Then they would take out the center spindle and pack more ice around the canister of ice cream until we were ready to dish it up—so cold it stung the roof of your mouth and so delicious you let it melt all the way down your throat instead of swallowing.

The county fair was a much bigger deal for the dairy club than the booth in which we had exhibited our sewing projects. Actually, we didn't have a real county fair, but the independent Hartford Fair served the same purpose. The older 4-Hers showing livestock lived in the barns with our animals, considering it a big adventure to roll into a blanket on some fresh straw for the night. It wasn't until the summer after eighth grade that I was allowed to stay. I remember Mother being shocked to hear that I had breakfasted on a hot dog and a pint of chocolate milk, but the offerings from the tents of food venders were limited and that seemed like a good choice to me.

We could, of course, have gone home—it was only twenty miles. In fact, we did take turns watering each other's livestock during the five-day fair so that you could go home for a bath and a good night's sleep before show day. But we had to be back early in the morning for the final grooming—brushing our calf's hair smooth and sponging off any dirty spots, polishing her hooves with black shoe polish, back combing her tail to make it fluff between her legs. The show ring was simply a grass field and each class usually had no more than six or eight animals but I was pleased to win a blue ribbon and a small cash prize.

The midway was small with rides like merry-go-rounds geared toward very young children, a few vendors with hot dogs and cotton candy, and booths to toss rings over the neck of a bottle to win a teddy bear. There was a racetrack that hosted harness racing one afternoon and drew the biggest crowds of the week. But mostly it was a junior fair for a couple of hundred 4-H members to show their calves or pigs or sheep and for their parents to help with the final grooming and visit nervously while awaiting the judge's decision.

Many of the dairy cattle were the popular Holsteins or Jerseys. Showing Ayrshires at the Hartford Fair guaranteed us a prize and that was fine with me.

14

Mairzy Doats

Mairzy doats and dozy doats
and liddle lamzy divey
a kiddley divey too, wouldn't you?

Our fat yellow school bus rocked with the rhythm as we belted out the words leaving a joyous trail of sound behind us in the coil of dust rising from the gravel road. Free from classes into a sunny autumn afternoon, we elementary school kids had no thought for Americans fighting their way across Europe and the Pacific Ocean. Our world was an island of innocence in a world at war.

Teachers and parents shook their heads and complained that the tune made no sense at all. Precisely the point. It didn't have to make sense to them.

If the words sound queer, and funny to your ear
a little bit jumbled and jivey,
Sing mares eat oats, and does eat oats,
and little lambs eat ivy

It was our song and we jived at the top of our lungs. Adults weren't supposed to understand.

Riding the school bus for an hour or so each morning and evening to reach the Newark Township School was my first awareness that kids have a world of their own, and it was up to me, not my parents, to negotiate my place in it.

I remember so clearly the day a number of years ago when I began thinking this might have been the most important thing I ever learned in school. It began with a conversation with my granddaughter after picking her up from school.

"It was mystery meat again, and yucky peas." My granddaughter's shoulders shuddered with the intense distaste only a fifth grader can muster as she plays the sympathy card for an extra after-school cookie.

Knowing full well that I should not start this conversation, I replied, "You should be glad you have a school cafeteria. Grandma's school didn't even have one, and I had to take sandwiches and a thermos of milk in a metal lunch box."

For a moment she looked me right in the eye, and said with great seriousness. "Grandma, you didn't miss a thing."

Perhaps not. Maybe my 1940s childhood on Sharon View Farm was richer than I realized at the time.

I was a little more than a month shy of my sixth birthday when I took the momentous and eagerly anticipated step of entering the first grade at the Newark Township School. We rural kids never heard of kindergarten although I know now that it was already available in many city districts. Our township school offered first through eighth grades in a four-room building erected some twenty years before I arrived there. Each room contained two grades—first and second, third and fourth, fifth and sixth, with the male teacher of the seventh and eighth grade room also serving as the building principal responsible to the county superintendent.

The two-story neo-classical building, with entries on either end accented by pilasters and pediments, had stairs to a hallway linking the two classrooms on each floor. The boys' restrooms were on one floor and girls on the other, the principal's office on the upper floor adjoining the seventh and eighth grade classroom had a teacher's lounge beneath it. A raised basement with windows at ground level contained a gymnasium that was used by the boys' basketball team and for recess when the weather prevented outside activities. A stage at one end made it usable as an auditorium for assemblies of the entire school and special events like graduation.

Sixty years later, on a summer day with no children around, I walked through this building. It is now part of a K-4 elementary complex of two dozen classrooms that includes an attached modern building larger than the original and portable classrooms for a burgeoning population within the Newark city limits.

I interrupted a janitor polishing floors, telling him I had attended this school. I was astonished to hear him claim that it was originally an eight room building, including the four-room addition to the north side of this building as part of the original. I realized that the architects had planned so carefully for its expansion to an eight-room building that its current occupants believe that it was always so. There was no way I could convince him that in my student days in the 1940s there were only four rooms. He insisted I must not be remembering correctly.

I peered into a classroom sniffing for that distinctive aroma of sweaty bodies, oiled wooden floors and chalky dust, but something wasn't right. Ah yes, the wooden floors are now smooth tile. As the janitor moved on with his work I had a strong desire to pat the side of the hall and assure the building that I did indeed remember its youth as a four-room school. Imagine me, like one of Charles Schultz's Peanuts gang talking to a school building!

But I really would have liked to ask the building how it feels about the cars streaming through the drive-through window for hamburgers at the fast food restaurant across the road. In my time, that was a swamp that yielded insects and frogs for our science projects. My visit was during summer vacation and I saw no students, but I left wondering whether we or they were surrounded by the more enriching environment.

I wish I could remember something significant about my experiences in Mrs. Nichols' first and second grade. I have a class picture and can identify myself as the fourth from the left in the center row, but I can't remember any names. I'm shocked to see that of the thirty-one students, twenty-seven were girls and only four boys. I don't remember that and I have no idea why it would have been so.

Mrs. Nichol's 1ˢᵗ & 2ⁿᵈ Grade, Newark Twp. School

I think I spent most of my time reading the entire collection of books in the small bookcase beneath the windows while most of the class learned the alphabet and sounded out words by their syllables. As far back as I can remember Mother read stories to us before bedtime, *Goldie Locks and the Three Bears, Little Black Sambo, Jack and the*

Beanstalk, Cinderella. I soon knew them by heart and would beg to read them myself. Reading was a magic power that I realized very early held the key to the world.

I loved to pretend to read the newspaper to Mother as she worked in the kitchen. She never knew how or when I learned to read, but told me that one day when I was five she picked up the paper I had been pretending to read and was surprised to find the story was actually there—plus some big words I skipped because I didn't understand them. I had probably been following her finger as she read us bedtime stories.

She soon tired of answering questions about all the words I didn't know and got a dictionary for the shelf where the salt and pepper shakers rested above our kitchen table so I could look them up myself. By the time I was in the third or fourth grade, she added a thesaurus and we played games to see who could name the most synonyms for any new word we discovered. Mother, not school, helped me develop a vocabulary that served me well in a career that required quite a bit of writing and public speaking.

Math was Daddy's domain, but I found it far less interesting. I remember learning to count the pigeons on the roof of the barn, and then to add or subtract as they arrived or flew away. He would challenge me. "If you count eight pigeons and two fly away, how many are left?" At first I simply counted them again and couldn't figure how Daddy knew without counting, but eventually it all became clear.

School was rather tame by comparison. But there were challenges, too. Spelling was hard and I hated to memorize words that weren't spelled the way they sounded. For years, every Friday afternoon in every grade our teacher would hold a spelling bee. The entire class formed a line in front of the room and she went down the line giving each student a word to spell. If you missed you had to sit down at your desk and, of course, it was quite an honor to be the last one standing. No matter how hard I tried I very rarely succeeded, although I usually managed to be among the last four or five. What a blessing it was when nearly five decades later I acquired a word processing program with a spell checker!

Another difficulty for me was music. Our school did not have a music teacher, but in the third and fourth grade Mrs. Emler was supposed to teach us the basics of musical scales, notes and clefs. I enjoyed listening to music or singing, but my voice was an alto—or perhaps a tenor if girls had been allowed that option. "Do, re, mi, fa, so, la, ti, do" at the teacher's pitch usually left me unable to reach a note or two at the high end. Even the boys whose voices had not yet changed could do better.

This was important because Mrs. Emler drew the outline of a tree on the blackboard and we made apples out of red construction paper and printed our names on them. If you completed the scale correctly you were allowed to attach your apple to one of the branches, but if not, your apple had to lay on the ground. Even though I liked Mrs. Emler and she regarded me as a good student, I wonder now why she never considered the possibility of my beginning the scale a few notes lower. It was my first experience in being expected to follow rules that had no rational basis.

Grammar was a different story. I think it was also in the third grade that we began to diagram simple sentences—subject, verb, object. Mrs. Emler would call us up to the blackboard in groups and check our work for accuracy. I loved it when we began to add adjectives and adverbs and then modifying phrases that you could dangle until your diagram was running into the space of the person beside you. This was intricate work, as much fun as finding the pieces to a jigsaw puzzle. When we were finished it was a real treat to be one of the two or three pupils chosen to take the dusty erasers outside and clap them together until they were reasonably chalk free—entrusted to be outside alone without a teacher telling us what to do.

Mrs. Emler's 3rd & 4th Grade, Newark Township

I ponder over a picture of that third and fourth grade class—twenty girls and eight boys—and I immediately notice the dresses. We girls all look like we are dressed for Easter Sunday! Girls wore cotton print dresses with Peter Pan or sailor collars, neat white bobby socks with oxfords or saddle shoes. We all have our hair neatly combed and held back with barrettes. The boys wear cotton shirts with open collars and several sport suspenders. Of course we were dressed for picture day, but we did wear dresses every day and our appearance reflects a time that valued neatness and conformity above individuality. Fourth from the left in the front row, my posture reveals how uncomfortable I feel in a body that has begun to grow into an awkward teenager.

Our desks were bolted to the floor, three rows across, and we all had assigned seats facing the teacher's desk. Attention deficit disorder or dyslexia had never been diagnosed, and it would be many years before many varied learning styles were acknowledged. We were not expected to leave our desk without permission nor to speak without raising our hand. Education in our school came in one size fits all.

I think it was that same year that I got my first big box of Crayolas.

Thirty-two marvelous crayons in rows that tantalized me not just with red and blue but with choices between scarlet or crimson, indigo or azure. And I loved their smooth points—although from past experience with boxes of eight I knew they would be broken stubs before the year was well under way.

We had no art teacher, but our classroom teachers regularly produced outlines of flowers and animals on the ditto machine in the school office and we were rewarded for coloring inside the pale purple outlines and getting the colors right for the subject. Cows were brown and grass was green, neither, of course, were ever orange or lavender. I'm sure our teachers had never seen and would have been shocked by a Miro or Picasso painting.

At the end of the third grade Mrs. Emler talked to my parents about letting me skip the fourth grade, knowing that I had watched and listened to them recite their lessons all year and would be bored to repeat it. But my parents felt—rightly, I suspect—that I was young for my class and needed more social experience or I would be uncomfortable by the time I reached high school. We compromised by letting me read if I finished my work ahead of the others, or serve as her helper with the third grade.

Social skills evolved on the playground and I suspect I am not unusual in remembering those scenes more vividly than the classroom. The playground beside our school had a small merry-go-round with a wooden seat that accommodated ten or twelve children who grabbed hold and ran and pushed to get it going as fast as possible before jumping on. It was too low for the biggest kids and too scary for the littlest but from about third through fifth grade it was a challenge to see who could be the last to jump on without losing hold and spinning off onto the grass nearby.

There was a wooden teeter-totter that you had to watch out for splinters, with three metal notches underneath that you could jump over the bar to compensate for one person being bigger than the other. It was important to ride this with a friend because some of the boys would plant their feet on the ground and hold you high up in the air and laugh when you screamed to come down. And there were six or eight swings that little kids needed a push to get started but bigger kids pumped their legs to fly as high as possible.

In the driveway where our school bus pulled up to unload, we girls jumped rope and played endless games of jacks. The baseball diamond was used for various games at recess—a mid-morning break that was divided into separate times for fourth grade and younger and fifth grade and older, with one unlucky teacher in charge. We usually played games like Crack the Whip with a couple of the bigger boys leading and little kids left to tumble off the end. My friends and I would lock arms around each other's waists and try to get a place in the middle. Or we formed two lines for Red Rover—Red Rover, Red Rover, let _____ (and everyone held their breath to see if they would be the chosen one) come over."

The seventh and eighth grade girls had a softball team that played teams from other township schools in the fall after school. When I watched the Little League games of my grandchildren, I would smile ironically at their piles of gear, remembering our single bat and ball, no special shoes or uniforms. Perhaps because I liked the action and had a throwing arm that could reach second base, I played catcher—without face mask or protective pads, but as I recall without serious bruises and certainly no broken bones. When I was in the eighth grade we won five games and lost seven, better than the boys' team that won two and lost ten.

Our coach was Miss Twyford, a new teacher that year for the fifth and sixth grade. She was just out of college—a real treat for those of us who had known only middle-aged women teachers—and pretty! A couple of times her boyfriend came to our games and he was so handsome we all became too nervous to catch or hit the ball.

And wonder of wonders, she drove a convertible, the first one we had ever seen.

I remember several of us being packed in with the top down for a ride to one of our away games and thinking we had died and gone to heaven. She knew just how to let up on the accelerator at the crest of a hill to make your stomach drop just like the roller coasters none of us had ever ridden. I don't believe any of us told our parents about that. For the first time we had a teacher who related more to us than to our parents, and she became a tantalizing model of the desirable women we girls might soon become.

Despite the carefree nature of my memories, I was in the second grade when Pearl Harbor was bombed, in the fifth when Germany surrendered. I try hard to recall what our teachers told us about the war and realize that most of what I know was acquired later in high school, college, and through contacts with veterans. I don't remember any of my friends having fathers or brothers in the service.

But I do remember our sense of patriotism that even we children should do what we could for the war effort. We brought dimes to school each week and put them in slotted cardboard folders until we had enough to buy an E Bond. And we held a huge scrap drive with the promise of a prize for the room that collected the biggest pile. Our farm was a perfect source—rusty hoes that had lost their handles, pieces of barbed wire fence that my father was glad to have picked up before they were mistakenly swallowed by a cow, dented aluminum pans or rusty iron skillets Mother no longer used. Dave and I were so competitive I think Daddy had to rescue a few tools that he really needed to keep. We had all been indoctrinated with patriotic fever and our class shouted "Use it up, wear it out, make it do, or do without."

But the thing I remember most vividly about the war effort is an activity that some historians say never happened. The fall that I was in the fourth grade our school bus overflowed with burlap bags of milkweed pods, their fuzzy seed-bearing floss escaping all over our bus, all over our classrooms, all over our clothes. Why? Germans had captured the Indonesian islands that were the source of the Kapok floss used in life jackets. Milkweed floss was chosen as a substitute and school kids were recruited to gather the wild milkweed that grew all over Ohio to be used in making life jackets. We scoured the roadsides and pastures where milkweed grew abundantly, and if our school was typical, students must have collected enough milkweed seeds to blanket the entire ocean. But some historians say that milkweed was never actually used to manufacture life jackets for downed pilots. It was simply one of the government's propaganda efforts to mobilize public sentiment for the war effort.

My elementary school years were lived under the clouds of war, and yet today I watch television as students are terrified by a gun-wielding classmate and I remember my schooldays as an innocent time. Perhaps it was my childhood comprehension that protected my optimism, or maybe teachers and parents united to protect us from the realities of terror more successfully in that pre-television era than is possible today. Certainly, those of us who had no close relative in combat felt patriotically involved but emotionally removed from the horrors of war.

My mother, like many, was a proud saver of school treasures their children little appreciated. To her I am indebted for a copy of the *Newark Township Annual* which I had completely forgotten existed although in the eighth grade I am listed as its editor. The faded purple letters from our school's ditto (duplication) machine have somehow survived on its construction paper cover for more than half a century. Among letters to the editor, one signed "A Wishful Thinker" spoke "As one of the girls who has been politely kicked out of the gymnasium while boys basketball practice is underway, I say it is time to face the fact that girls like fun too and need space." I do hope she lived long enough to see her granddaughters benefit from Title X.

Another from "A Knowledge Seeker" called for the creation of a school library containing reference and fiction books as well as magazines, pointing out "It is quite inconvenient to interrupt a classroom to borrow a *Book of Knowledge* or an *Atlas*." Although our resources were limited, the P.T.A. held a fund raising fall festival with bingo games, ice cream, a bazaar, and a fish pond that netted enough to purchase a bicycle rack, scales, Christmas decorations and drapes for the principal's office.

I had forgotten about the Leap Year party held by the seventh and eighth-grade girls until I began reading about the balloons and crepe paper streamers strung across the gym and the red cellophane wrapped around the cages that protected the ceiling lights from basketballs. Then it all began to come back. I had invited Tommy Beckett, who was a couple of inches shorter than I—as seventh and eighth grade boys were prone to be. The bunny hop was popular that year and we danced to records and played a variety of games that I am certain included spin the bottle with much giggling and a few innocent kisses. According to our student paper the party ended with homemade fudge, bursting balloons, and at 10:30 PM everyone singing *Now is the Hour*. My first official date!

That same year the school board supplied the school with a movie projector so movies from the Ohio Department of Education could be shown every Thursday afternoon. These were mostly short travelogues, or historical and geographical films, but on a few occasions there were full length classics like *Swiss Family Robinson*—the first movie I ever saw since our family never attended the theater in Newark. At the end of the school year we voted for our favorite movie stars, and chose actresses June Allyson and Dale Evans, actors Peter Lawford and Roy Rogers.

One of the year's highlights for Mr. Dixon's eighth grade civics class was a trip to the county courthouse where we toured county offices such as the recorder, auditor, engineer, and commissioners. I suspect we heard explanations of their responsibilities that went right in one ear and out the other, but the highlight was sitting in the big courtroom trimmed with gilt and hearing the Juvenile Court judge explain different types of crime and how sentences were determined. That made quite an impression, but innocents that we were none of us knew anyone who had been arrested for a crime. We were eons removed from drugs and gangs and guns.

The war had ended and gas rationing was but a memory that spring as we prepared for the big event—out class trip to Coney Island! None of us had been to this amusement park near Cincinnati and we buzzed with excitement over plans for the daylong trip in our school bus. I'm sure we had chaperones—but not my parents! We must have sung most of the way.

Give me land, lots of land under starry skies above

Don't fence me in!

I'm sure we tried most of the rides, but the one I remember best was one that had wheels on a large wheel that spun in opposite direction, an intensified version our games of crack the whip. Two of my friends and I screamed so loudly that the operator extended our ride for a couple of free rounds. We were great advertising!

This phase of my childhood ended at graduation in the school gym on a warm May evening. There were nineteen in our eighth-grade class and we girls wore white dresses with my first medium high heels and hose that I tugged and pulled to assure the seam ran straight up the back of my legs. Each of the girls had a red rose proudly pinned at the shoulder—upside down—while the boys wore their rose on their jackets right side up. Could that have been decided by the same etiquette expert who decreed that men would move forward and women backward when dancing?

Newark Township 8th grade graduation, 1948

I felt a mixture of pride and embarrassment receiving my diploma from my father who was serving as president of the Newark Township School Board—and being a couple of inches taller in my new heels.

My friends Tommy Beckett and Glenna Lee played piano and accordion solos, and I was one of the two class speakers. How I cringe now as I read the clichés, "We are going on. We would not stay nor would you have us, yet the old ties are strong. We do not want to break them but rather to lengthen them the more." Totally naive but supremely confident thirteen and fourteen-year-olds, we stood poised on the diving board eager jump in and experience life.

Ellis Evans, Newark Township School Board President,
presenting her eighth grade diploma, 1948

Printed in the United States
by Baker & Taylor Publisher Services